THE AUGSBURG CONFESSION

THE CONCORDIA READER'S EDITION

Excerpted from the Book of Concord in
Concordia: The Lutheran Confessions

Available from Concordia Publishing House
800-325-3040 or cph.org/concordia

CONCORDIA PUBLISHING HOUSE • SAINT LOUIS

Published 2013 Concordia Publishing House
3558 S. Jefferson Ave., St. Louis, MO 63118-3968
1-800-325-3040 · www.cph.org

Edited by Paul T. McCain

Rev. Matthew C. Harrison Private Collection, pages 11, 12, 18, 24, 25, 43.
The Complete Woodcuts of Albrecht Dürer, edited by Willi Kurth (New York: Arden Book Company, 1936, page 20.
The Smithey Collection of Reformation Works, Pritzlaff Memorial Library Rare Book Collection: Concordia Seminary Library, St. Louis, Missouri, page 29.

Manufactured in the United States of America

6 7 8 9 10   22 21 20 19 18 17

⟨ⁿⁿⁿ⟩

USER'S GUIDE

Article number ⟶ ARTICLE IX

Article heading ⟶ **Baptism**

────ⁿⁿ────

Annotation by the editor ⟶ Note: The Bible teaches that Baptism is a gift of God's grace by which He applies the benefits of Christ's life, death, and resurrection to us personally. Because all people are conceived and born in sin, we all need salvation. Because Baptism is God's way of bringing us salvation, infants should also be baptized. During the Reformation, as now, some Christian groups turned Baptism from God's saving activity into an act of Christian obedience. This view of Baptism arises from the denial of original sin and a semi-Pelagian view of salvation, whereby faith becomes the good work we contribute. This article concentrates on what God gives in this Sacrament.

Confessional article begins

Marginal number

────ⁿⁿ────

‹ › Wording provided from a translation (in this case, a German document is clarified by wording from the Latin translation; each document's introduction describes its German or Latin base text; e.g., p. 34).

1   Concerning Baptism, our churches teach that Baptism is necessary for salvation [Mark 16:16] and that God's grace is offered
2   through Baptism [Titus 3:4–7]. They teach that children are to be baptized [Acts 2:38–39]. Being offered to God through Baptism, they are received into God's grace.

[ ] Reference or wording provided by an editor

3   Our churches condemn the Anabaptists, who reject the Baptism of children, and say that children are saved without Baptism.

V D M A

Verbum Domini Manet in Aeternum

The Word of the Lord Endures Forever

Verbum Domini Manet in Aeternum is the motto of the Lutheran Reformation, a confident expression of the enduring power and authority of God's Word. The motto is based on 1 Peter 1:24–25. It first appeared in the court of Frederick the Wise in 1522. He had it sewn onto the right sleeve of the court's official clothing, which was worn by prince and servant alike. It was used by Frederick's successors, his brother John the Steadfast, and his nephew John Frederick the Magnanimous. It became the official motto of the Smalcaldic League and was used on flags, banners, swords and uniforms as symbol of unity of the Lutheran laity who struggled to defend their beliefs, communities, families, and lives against those who were intent on destroying them.

THE CONFESSION OF FAITH

⟨THE AUGSBURG CONFESSION⟩

which was submitted to
His Imperial Majesty Charles V at the
Imperial Meeting of Augsburg
in the Year 1530
⟨by certain princes and cities⟩

*I will also speak of Your testimonies before kings
and shall not be put to shame.*

Psalm 119:46

The Wise Men Adore Christ

During the Imperial Meeting [Diet] of Augsburg, Lutheran princes confessed their faith boldly before the most powerful leaders of Europe. The powerful and mighty are always most wise when they bow in humble adoration before Christ.

Editor's Introduction to the Augsburg Confession

Against the gates of hell, with the grace and help of God.

—Layman Gregory Brück

On Saturday, June 25, 1530, at three o'clock in the afternoon, Dr. Christian Beyer stood, walked toward the Emperor of the Holy Roman Empire, Charles V, and began reading the Augsburg Confession in a loud and distinct voice. Through the open windows a hushed crowd outside in the courtyard hung on his every word, as did the two hundred or so people gathered in the hall. Beside Dr. Beyer stood Dr. Gregory Brück, holding a copy of the Augsburg Confession in Latin. The German princes around them stood up to indicate their support for the Confession. The emperor motioned for them to sit down.

When Dr. Beyer finished reading, Dr. Brück took the German copy of the Confession from him, handed both copies to the emperor, and said, "Most gracious Emperor, this is a Confession that will even prevail against the gates of hell, with the grace and help of God." Thus was the Augsburg Confession presented as a unique Confession of the truth of God's holy Word, distinct from Romanism on the one hand, and Reformed, Anabaptists, and radicals on the other. June 25, 1530, is a date every bit as important for Lutherans as is the more familiar date of October 31, 1517—the day on which Luther posted his Ninety-five Theses.

Events Leading to Augsburg

The presentation of the Augsburg Confession was a decisive moment, one long in coming. It is important to understand the history leading up to the Imperial Meeting at Augsburg. Nine years earlier, on April 18, 1521, at the Imperial Meeting in Worms, Charles had listened as Martin Luther refused to recant his teachings, saying, "I cannot and will not recant. I cannot do otherwise. Here I stand. God help me. Amen." Now Charles was watching as the most important rulers in his German territories confessed their faith openly and courageously in spite of the threats to their lives from both the government and the Church.

Martin Luther had been declared a criminal and a heretic; he was excommunicated and sentenced to death in April of 1521. By 1526, the Reformation had spread to the point that during an Imperial Meeting at Speyer, the Lutheran princes forced through a resolution that gave each of them the right to arrange religious matters in their respective territories—in any way he felt was best—until the emperor was able to have the pope call a General Council of the Church. So from 1526 to 1529, little changed in the Holy Roman Empire. As a result, most of Northern Germany became Lutheran, along with many cities in Southern Germany. At the second

Imperial Meeting in Speyer (1529), the princes loyal to Rome reversed the decision made three years earlier. The princes loyal to the Lutheran Reformation and other reforming movements fiercely protested this decision, issuing a formal *Protestio*. Thus the Lutherans, along with other reformers, were labeled *Protestants*. The name has stuck ever since.

Charles ordered all rulers within the Empire to go to Augsburg to attend the Imperial Meeting (also known as a *Reichstag* or a *Diet*). He wanted to settle, once and for all, the controversies in the churches throughout his Germany. The armies of the Turkish Empire were literally at the eastern gates of Charles's Empire. He wanted unity so that the Turkish threat could be met. He hoped that a combination of kindness, cajoling, and finally, threats, would stop the Lutheran movement and restore Romanism throughout the Empire. But things did not go as Charles had hoped.

The Schwabach, Marburg, and Torgau Articles

Lutheranism was only tolerated where it could not be eliminated by military force. Lutherans had no protection in German territories that were loyal to Rome. After the 1529 Diet of Speyer, Philip of Hesse sought to create a political federation for the mutual defense of those who had protested the autocratic action of Charles V. Philip of Hesse and Jacob Sturm united Saxony and Hesse with certain Southern German evangelical cities (with Ulm, Strasbourg, and Nürnberg as the nucleus). The coalition was created on April 22, 1529, in a secret agreement at Speyer. To clear the way for possible inclusion of the Swiss in the federation, Philip of Hesse planned to settle the dispute between Luther and Ulrich Zwingli at a meeting at Philip's castle in Marburg.

The Lutherans were concerned by Philip of Hesse's desire to put political unity ahead of doctrinal unity. After the Diet of Speyer, Philip Melanchthon (who had kept silent regarding differences between the German Lutherans and the Swiss) had a change of heart and tried to thwart the federation. Luther also opposed a federation without confessional unity. The Schwabach Articles were prepared by Luther and others sometime between July 25 and September 14 of that year.

The Marburg Colloquy took place October 2–4, 1529. Ulrich Zwingli and Martin Luther faced each other across a table for most of the meeting. The two groups identified much that they agreed about, yet the talks broke down. The disagreement had to do with the Lord's Supper. Zwingli was willing to settle for an "agreement to disagree" approach, but Luther insisted that Jesus' words "This is My body" mean "This *is* My body." In fact, he took a piece of chalk and wrote the words "This is My body" on the table itself (*Hoc est Corpus Meum*). Whenever Zwingli or the other Swiss Reformers tried to disagree with Luther about the reality of those words, Luther would lift the tablecloth and point to the words. The Marburg Articles therefore indicate "We are not agreed as to whether the true body and blood of Christ are bodily present in the bread and wine."

The Marburg Articles, along with the Schwabach Articles, provided a firm foundation for the writing of the Augsburg Confession. The seventeen Schwabach

Articles were first presented on October 16, 1529. They insisted on unity in doctrine as a prerequisite for any cooperation among the various Protestant groups in Germany.

Charles V persisted with his efforts to eliminate the religious controversies in his territories. He was facing pressure from the threat of a Turkish invasion from the East. He was also mindful that the pope might, at any time, strike an alliance with the ruler of France and attack his Empire from the West. The Empire was a coalition of relatively independent territories and free cities. The key rulers of the Empire were known as "electors," for they actually elected the emperor. Charles depended on them both militarily and politically. He could not afford to alienate them. Charles was very devout and felt strongly that it was his duty to protect the Roman Church from the threat posed by the Lutherans and other Protestant reformers. He hoped that the meeting at Augsburg would settle all disputes.

The elector of Saxony, John the Steadfast, at first refused to attend the meeting in Augsburg. But Charles urged him to do so. Since Charles invited everyone attending to share their "opinions, thoughts, and notions," Elector John asked the Wittenberg theologians, led by Martin Luther, to prepare a statement of confession. Martin Luther, Philip Melanchthon, Justas Jonas, and John Bugenhagen met in Torgau and went to work immediately. Their document was given to Elector John at the Torgau Castle in March of 1530, and is therefore known as the Torgau Articles.

Philip Melanchthon (1497–1560)

Philip Melanchthon was asked by the Elector to write a comprehensive statement of faith. He did so without close consultation with Luther, but he relied heavily on the Schwabach, Marburg, and Torgau Articles—each of which was very much a product of Martin Luther. Luther indicated he approved of Melanchthon's work, though he pointed out that he would never have been able "to tread as lightly" as Melanchthon did.

The Gathering at Augsburg

On April 4, Elector John left Torgau with Martin Luther, Philip Melanchthon, Justas Jonas, and Veit Dietrich (a secretary to Luther). Ten days later, on Good Friday, they arrived at Coburg Castle. Luther and the Elector remained at Coburg while the others traveled on to Augsburg. There, Philip Melanchthon was given the responsibility of leading the Lutheran theologians. (However, the Elector had set up a special courier service to make sure letters between Luther and his colleagues would be sent and received quickly.) Elector John arrived in Augsburg on May 2.

The meeting began with a clear signal that the courageous Lutheran laymen were not about to concede to the emperor's demands, nor compromise their convictions. As Charles's royal procession approached Augsburg, it was met by a large del-

Emperor Charles V (1500–58)

Charles V became Holy Roman Emperor on June 28, 1519, about two years after Martin Luther posted the Ninety-five Theses. For forty years Charles struggled against Lutheranism. This woodcut depicts him in Erlangen in 1532, two years after the Diet of Augsburg. In 1547 he captured Wittenberg. His knights wanted to desecrate Luther's grave. Charles explained that he made war against the living, not the dead. He relinquished his throne in 1558, having failed to exterminate Lutheranism in his lands. He died in a monastery in Spain, a lonely, broken man who had suffered emotionally, physically, and spiritually.

egation from the city, including the Lutheran princes. The pope's ambassador stood to give the whole assembly a special blessing from the pope. When the crowd knelt, Elector John and his fellow Lutheran princes refused to kneel. Charles and those with him made their way into the city and arrived at the cathedral, where a special Mass was held. The crowd noticed that again Elector John and Philip of Hesse refused to kneel and remained standing, with their heads covered, during the blessing.

Later that evening, Charles and his brother Ferdinand, the King of Austria, met privately with the Lutheran princes. They ordered them to forbid any Lutheran preaching in Augsburg during the meeting. They commanded them to attend the Corpus Christi festival the next day with the emperor. George, Margrave of Brandenburg, spoke boldly for the Lutherans. He refused to concede to Charles's demands, saying, "Before I let anyone take from me the Word of God and ask me to deny my God, I will kneel and let them strike off my head." The emperor, clearly taken aback by George's boldness, sputtered in broken German, "Not cut off head, dear prince. Not cut off head."

Writing the Augsburg Confession

The plan to present the Torgau Articles had to be scrapped when it was found out that a lengthy, slanderous attack on Luther had been prepared by John Eck—Luther's old nemesis. At Leipzig in 1519, it was Eck who had tried to brand Luther as a heretic. Now, he had secretly written a lengthy attack on Luther and his followers in a book titled *Four Hundred and Four Articles for the Diet in Augsburg.* It included quotations from Martin Luther's writings, as well as from other Protestant reformers.

The book was highly inaccurate and tried to equate the Lutherans with the teachings of Ulrich Zwingli and the most radical of all the reformers, known as the Anabaptists. Eck's goal was to identify Lutheranism with the most extreme reformers, some of whom denied the most basic doctrines of historic Christianity. In light of this development, the Lutherans were forced to prepare a new statement of faith and specifically distance themselves from Zwinglians, Anabaptists, and others.

The Augsburg Confession was intentionally crafted to present a gentle and peaceful response to the emperor. It was intended only to speak for Saxony. However, as various German leaders read it they indicated that they, too, wanted to sign their names and make it their Confession.

So on June 25, 1530, courageous Lutheran laymen confessed their faith and told the emperor and the Roman Church what they believed, taught, and confessed. They relied on the promise of God's Word, as contained in Psalm 119:46, "I will also speak of Your testimonies before kings and shall not be put to shame." The Augsburg Confession was presented as a statement of biblical truth and a proposal for true unity in the Christian faith. It has never been withdrawn.

The translation is from the 1584 Latin edition of the Book of Concord, which was the base text for the Augsburg Confession in the *Concordia Triglotta.* See the User's Guide on page 3 for details about the use of brackets and symbols.

TIMELINE

1521 Luther excommunicated by papal bull *Decet Romanum Pontificem*; appears before Diet of Worms; refuses to recant

Anabaptist Thomas Münzer begins preaching against infant Baptism

1524 Peasants' War begins, led in part by Thomas Münzer

1525 George Blaurock is rebaptized by Conrad Grebel; marks formal beginning of Anabaptist movement

Luther marries Katharina von Bora, June 13

1526 Diet of Speyer grants German princes right to establish religion in their territory

1529 Luther publishes *Small Catechism* and *Large Catechism*

Following Second Diet of Speyer, term *Protestant* used to refer to those who agree with Luther

Schwabach Articles drafted, July–September

Luther, Melanchthon, and Zwingli meet for Marburg Colloquy; unable to agree on Lord's Supper; Marburg Articles drafted

Turks unsuccessfully lay siege to Vienna

1530 Torgau Articles drafted, March

Augsburg Confession presented to Charles V at Diet of Augsburg, June 25

1531 *Augsburg Confession* and *Apology* published, April–May; *Apology's* second edition published, September

Ulrich Zwingli dies on Swiss battlefield at Kappel am Albis

OUTLINE

Preface to Emperor Charles V

I. God

II. Original Sin

III. The Son of God

IV. Justification

V. The Ministry

VI. New Obedience

VII. The Church

VIII. What the Church Is

IX. Baptism

X. The Lord's Supper

XI. Confession

XII. Repentance

XIII. The Use of the Sacraments

XIV. Order in the Church

XV. Church Ceremonies

XVI. Civil Government

XVII. Christ's Return for Judgment

XVIII. Free Will

XIX. The Cause of Sin

XX. Good Works

XXI. Worship of the Saints

   A Summary Statement

   A Review of the Various Abuses That Have Been Corrected

XXII. Both Kinds in the Sacrament

XXIII. The Marriage of Priests

XXIV. The Mass

XXV. Confession

XXVI. The Distinction of Meats

XXVII. Monastic Vows

XXVIII. Church Authority

Conclusion

THE AUGSBURG CONFESSION

Preface

To Emperor Charles V

1 Most invincible Emperor, Caesar Augustus, most clement Lord: Your Imperial Majesty has summoned a meeting of the Empire here at Augsburg to consider taking action against the Turk, discussing how best to stand effectively against his fury and attacks by means of military force. The Turk is the most atrocious and ancient hereditary enemy of the Christian name and religion. 2 This meeting is also to consider disagreements in our holy religion, the Christian faith, by hearing everyone's opinions and judgments in each other's presence. They are to be considered and evaluated among ourselves in mutual charity, mercy, and 3 kindness. After the removal and correction of things that either side has understood differently, these matters may be settled and brought back to one simple truth and 4 Christian concord. Then we may embrace and maintain the future of one pure and true religion under one Christ, doing battle under Him [Psalm 24:8], living in unity and concord in the one Christian Church.

5 We, the undersigned elector and princes, have been called to this gathering along with other electors, princes, and estates in obedient compliance with the Imperial mandate. Therefore, we have promptly come to Augsburg. We do not mean to boast when we say this, but we were among the first to be here.

6 At the very beginning of the meeting in Augsburg, Your Imperial Majesty made a proposal to the electors, princes, and other estates of the Empire. Among other things, you asked that the several estates of the Empire—on the strength of the Imperial edict—should submit their explanations, opinions, and judgments in German and Latin. On the 7 following Wednesday, we informed Your Imperial Majesty that after due deliberation we would present the articles of our Confession in one week. Therefore, concerning this 8 religious matter, we offer this Confession. It is ours and our preachers'. It shows, from the Holy Scriptures and God's pure Word, what has been up to this time presented in our lands, dukedoms, dominions, and cities, and taught in our churches.

In keeping with your edict, the other 9 electors, princes, and estates of the Empire may present similar writings, in Latin and German, giving their opinions in this religious matter. We, and those princes previously mentioned, are prepared to discuss, 10 in a friendly manner, all possible ways and means by which we may come together. We will do this in the presence of your Imperial Majesty, our most clement Lord. In this way, dissensions may be put away without offensive conflict. This can be done honorably, with God's help, so that we may be brought back to agreement and concord. As your edict shows, we are all under one 11 Christ and do battle under Him [Exodus 15:3]. We ought to confess the one Christ and do everything according to God's truth. With the most fervent prayers, this is what we ask of God.

However, regarding the rest of the electors, princes, and estates, who form the other 12 side: no progress may be made, nor any result achieved by this treatment of religious matters, as Your Imperial Majesty has wisely determined that it should be dealt with and treated, by mutual presentation of writings and calm conferring together among our-

13 selves. We will at least leave with you a clear testimony. We are not holding back from anything that could bring about Christian concord, such as could be effected with

14 God and a good conscience. Your Imperial Majesty—and the other electors and estates of the Empire, and all moved by sincere love and zeal for religion, who will give an impartial hearing to this matter—please graciously offer to take notice of this and to understand this from our Confession.

15   Your Imperial Majesty, has—not once but often—graciously pointed something out to the electors, princes, and estates of the Empire. At the meeting of Speyer (1526), according to the form of Your Imperial instruction and commission, this point

16 was given and prescribed. Your Imperial Majesty caused it to be stated and publicly proclaimed that Your Majesty—in dealing with this religious matter, for certain reasons that were alleged in Your Majesty's name— was not willing to decide and could not determine anything. But that Your Majesty would diligently use Your Majesty's office with the Roman Pontiff for the convening

17 of a General Council. The same matter was publicly set forth at greater length a year ago at the last meeting of the Empire, at Speyer.

18 There Your Imperial Majesty (through His Highness Ferdinand, King of Bohemia and Hungary, our friend and clement Lord, as well as through the Orator and Imperial Commissioners) caused the following to be submitted among other things: concerning the calling of a council, Your Imperial Majesty had taken notice of and has pondered, the resolution of (a) Your Majesty's Representative in the Empire, and of (b) the

President and Imperial Counselors, and (c) the Legates from other Estates convened at Ratisbon. Your Imperial Majesty also judged   19 that it was helpful to convene a Council. Your Imperial Majesty did not doubt that the Roman pontiff could be persuaded to hold a General Council. For the matters between Your Imperial Majesty and the Roman pontiff were nearing agreement and Christian reconciliation. Your Imperial Maj-   20 esty himself pointed out that he would work to secure the said chief pontiff's consent for convening a General Council, together with your Imperial Majesty, to be announced as soon as possible by letters that were to be sent out.

Therefore, if the outcome should be that   21 the differences between us and the other parties in this religious matter should not be settled with friendliness and charity, then here, before Your Imperial Majesty, we obediently offer, in addition to what we have already done, to appear and defend our cause in such a general, free Christian Council. There has always been harmonious action and agreement among the electors, princes, and other estates to hold a Council, in all the Imperial Meetings held during Your Majesty's reign. Even before   22 this time, we have appealed this great and grave matter, to the assembly of this General Council, and to your Imperial Majesty, in an appropriate manner. We still stand by   23 this appeal, both to your Imperial Majesty and to a Council. We have no intention to abandon our appeal, with this or any other document. This would not be possible, unless the matter between us and the other side is settled with friendliness and charity, resolved and brought to Christian harmony, according to the latest Imperial Citation. In regard to this appeal we sol-   24 emnly and publicly testify here.

John the Steadfast of Saxony (1468–1532)

John the Steadfast, brother of Frederick the Wise and father of John Frederick the Magnanimous, was the leader of the Lutheran princes and cities who gathered for the Diet of Augsburg. He well deserved to be called "Steadfast." He boldly confessed the truth of God's Word and risked everything rather than compromise and lose the Gospel of Jesus Christ.

Gregory Brück (1485–1557)

Courageous Lutheran layman, counselor and aide to Frederick the Wise. He wrote the preface and the conclusion of the Augsburg Confession. He stood with Christian Beyer as he publicly read the Augsburg Confession (June 25, 1530). Then Brück handed the German and Latin copies to the Emperor.

CHIEF ARTICLES OF FAITH

ARTICLE I

God

Note: Martin Luther never intended to start a new church, but rather to purify the one, holy, catholic, and apostolic Church. The Augsburg Confession strongly affirms the doctrine of the Trinity confessed at the Council of Nicaea (325), and later affirmed by the Council of Constantinople (381). God is one divine essence in three distinct persons—Father, Son, and Holy Spirit. The Scriptures reveal this great mystery, confessed by all Christians.

During the Reformation, radical groups espoused various forms of earlier heresies. The Augsburg Confession condemns the ancient heresies concerning God. Article I proves that Lutheranism is deeply anchored in the historic doctrine of biblical Christianity. It embraces the faith of the Church through the ages and rejects all the errors the Church has rejected.

---

1   Our churches teach with common consent that the decree of the Council of Nicaea about the unity of the divine essence and
2   the three persons is true. It is to be believed without any doubt. God is one divine essence who is eternal, without a body, without parts, of infinite power, wisdom, and goodness. He is the maker and preserver of all things, visible and invisible [Nehemiah
3   9:6]. Yet there are three persons, the Father, the Son, and the Holy Spirit [Matthew 28:19]. These three persons are of the same
4   essence and power. Our churches use the term *person* as the Fathers have used it. We use it to signify, not a part or quality in another, but that which subsists of itself.

5   Our churches condemn all heresies [Titus 3:10–11] that arose against this article, such as the Manichaeans, who assumed that there are two "principles," one Good and the other Evil. They also condemn the Valentinians, Arians, Eunomians, Muslims, and all heresies such as these. Our churches also
6   condemn the Samosatenes, old and new, who contend that God is but one person. Through sophistry they impiously argue that the Word and the Holy Spirit are not distinct persons. They say that *Word* signifies a spoken word, and *Spirit* signifies motion created in things.

ARTICLE II

Original Sin

Note: Sin is much more than thinking, saying, and doing things that are wrong. It is a terminal disease. We are all conceived and born in sin; we inherit it from our first parents, Adam and Eve. The disease of sin can be overcome, but only by one medicine: the cleansing, healing, and forgiving blood of God's own Son. By rejecting Pelagian errors in Article II, the Augsburg Confession subtly refers to the Roman view of sin. The Roman Church taught and still teaches that concupiscence (the inborn inclination to sin) is not actually sin. By misdiagnosing our fatal illness, Rome leads people to believe they are able to cooperate with God's grace for salvation. Lutheranism rejects all teachings that imply we are responsible for or contribute to our salvation.

---

1   Our churches teach that since the fall of Adam [Romans 5:12], all who are naturally born are born with sin [Psalm 51:5], that is, without the fear of God, without trust in God, and with the inclination to sin, called concupiscence. Concupiscence is a disease   2

and original vice that is truly sin. It damns and brings eternal death on those who are not born anew through Baptism and the Holy Spirit [John 3:5].

3   Our churches condemn the Pelagians and others who deny that original depravity is sin, thus obscuring the glory of Christ's merit and benefits. Pelagians argue that a person can be justified before God by his own strength and reason.

ARTICLE III

The Son of God

Note: The Augsburg Confession teaches the historic, biblical doctrine of Christ. Many early controversies about Christ's human and divine natures were resolved through careful study of God's Word, and are reflected in the Nicene Creed. Article III echoes that creed—our Lord Jesus Christ is one person having two natures: truly God and truly man. This is another mystery of the Christian faith that we receive with thanks, bowing before Christ in humble adoration. His incarnation in the womb of His virgin mother, Mary, was for our salvation. He is, and remains, for all eternity the God-man, the One who appeased, or propitiated, God's wrath against our sin and won for us eternal life. Even now He is present with us through His appointed means of grace—the Gospel and the Sacraments. He comes to strengthen, sustain, and support us, and to bring us safely to our heavenly home.

1   Our churches teach that the Word, that is, the Son of God [John 1:14], assumed the human nature in the womb of the Blessed
2   Virgin Mary. So there are two natures—the divine and the human—inseparably joined in one person. There is one Christ, true God and true man, who was born of the Virgin Mary, truly suffered, was crucified, died, and was buried. He did this to reconcile the   3 Father to us and to be a sacrifice, not only for original guilt, but also for all actual sins of mankind [John 1:29].

He also descended into hell, and truly   4 rose again on the third day. Afterward, He ascended into heaven to sit at the right hand of the Father. There He forever reigns and has dominion over all creatures. He sancti-   5 fies those who believe in Him, by sending the Holy Spirit into their hearts to rule, comfort, and make them alive. He defends them against the devil and the power of sin.

The same Christ will openly come again   6 to judge the living and the dead, and so forth, according to the Apostles' Creed.

ARTICLE IV

Justification

Note: There is a historic saying in Lutheranism that the Church stands or falls on the article of justification. To justify means "to declare righteous." God's sure and certain declaration that we are righteous in His eyes is possible only because of our Savior, Jesus Christ. Through His life, Jesus satisfied God's demand for perfect obedience. Through His sacrificial death, Jesus took God's wrath and atoned for the sins of the world. The Holy Spirit, through the means of grace, works in us saving faith, which personally apprehends what Christ has done for us. Our justification before God, therefore, is brought about by the One who lived, suffered, and died for our salvation. We cannot merit God's favor through our obedience; we cannot offer sacrifices to pay for our sins. But what we cannot do for ourselves, Christ has done for us. He is the solid Rock on which God builds His Church. On Him, and Him alone, we stand forgiven.

1   Our churches teach that people cannot be justified before God by their own
2 strength, merits, or works. People are freely justified for Christ's sake, through faith, when they believe that they are received into favor and that their sins are forgiven for Christ's sake. By His death, Christ made sat-
3 isfaction for our sins. God counts this faith for righteousness in His sight (Romans 3 and 4 [3:21–26; 4:5]).

ARTICLE V
The Ministry

Note: How can what Christ did for us two thousand years ago—through His life, death, and resurrection—become effective in our lives today? During the Reformation, as also today, some imagined they would experience the Holy Spirit through their own reflections, by enjoying nature, or by ecstatic religious experiences. The comforting truth is that the Holy Spirit works through objective, external, sure, and certain means of grace, through which we receive justification by grace alone, through faith alone, on account of Christ alone. While the most direct concern of Article V is to confess the Holy Spirit's work through the means of grace, there is also in view, indirectly, the Office of the Ministry, which the German version of the Augsburg Confession calls "the Preaching Office" [das Predigtamt]. The Preaching Office is not instituted by man, but is established by God Himself. Article XIV discusses the necessity of the Church call.

1   So that we may obtain this faith, the ministry of teaching the Gospel and administer-
2 ing the Sacraments was instituted. Through the Word and Sacraments, as through in-
struments, the Holy Spirit is given [John 20:22]. He works faith, when and where it pleases God [John 3:8], in those who hear the good news that God justifies those who 3 believe that they are received into grace for Christ's sake. This happens not through our own merits, but for Christ's sake.

Our churches condemn the Anabaptists 4 and others who think that through their own preparations and works the Holy Spirit comes to them without the external Word.

ARTICLE VI
New Obedience

Note: Lutherans are sometimes accused of denying that Christians should do good works. The article on new obedience follows on the heels of the articles on justification and the ministry, and clearly states that Lutherans do insist on good works. The faith given by the Holy Spirit is a living and active power in our lives, bearing the fruit of good works. We must do good works. God commands them. However, they do not save us. They are always the result of saving faith. This article refers to an Early Church Father as proof that this teaching is anchored in the Church's historic teaching and practice.

Our churches teach that this faith is 1 bound to bring forth good fruit [Galatians 5:22–23]. It is necessary to do good works commanded by God [Ephesians 2:10], because of God's will. We should not rely on those works to merit justification before God. The forgiveness of sins and justification 2 is received through faith. The voice of Christ testifies, "So you also, when you have done all that you were commanded, say, 'We are unworthy servants; we have only done what was our duty'" (Luke 17:10). The Fathers 3 teach the same thing. Ambrose says, "It is ordained of God that he who believes in Christ is saved, freely receiving forgiveness of sins, without works, through faith alone."

ARTICLE VII
The Church

Note: Article VII has been rightly called the evangelical Magna Carta of the Lutheran Church. It cuts through the clutter of man-made ceremonies that had accumulated by the sixteenth century, focuses on the very heart of the matter, and defines church with eloquent simplicity. Outward unity in the Church is shaped, defined, and normed by biblical truth (teaching), not the other way around. Church fellowship is common participation in the saving treasures of the Church: Christ's gifts, His Gospel, and His Sacraments. Not any "Gospel" will do, but only that Gospel which is purely taught alongside correctly administered Sacraments (as noted in the German version).

1   Our churches teach that one holy Church is to remain forever. The Church is the congregation of saints [Psalm 149:1] in which the Gospel is purely taught and the Sacra-
2 ments are correctly administered. For the true unity of the Church it is enough to agree about the doctrine of the Gospel and the
3 administration of the Sacraments. It is not necessary that human traditions, that is, rites or ceremonies instituted by men, should be
4 the same everywhere. As Paul says, "One Lord, one faith, one baptism, one God and Father of all" (Ephesians 4:5–6).

ARTICLE VIII
What the Church Is

Note: This article elaborates on Article VII and makes it clear that the Church consists only of believers in Christ, those made holy by His mercy. Hypocrites are not in this sense any part of the Church. One may think of the term *church* in a broad and narrow sense. The Church, broadly speaking, is all those who assemble around Word and Sacrament. Narrowly speaking, the Church encompasses only believers. There are not two churches, one "visible" and one "invisible." Rather, we understand that here on the earth the Church is hidden because faith, or spiritual life, is "hidden with Christ in God" (Colossians 3:3). This hidden Church has public, visible marks, by which it is recognized with absolute certainty: Christ's Gospel and Sacraments, purely preached and administered.

1   Strictly speaking, the Church is the congregation of saints and true believers. However, because many hypocrites and evil persons are mingled within them in this life [Matthew 13:24–30], it is lawful to use Sacraments administered by evil men, according to the saying of Christ, "The scribes and the Pharisees sit on Moses' seat" (Mat-
2 thew 23:2). Both the Sacraments and Word are effective because of Christ's institution and command, even if they are administered by evil men.

3   Our churches condemn the Donatists, and others like them, who deny that it is lawful to use the ministry of evil men in the Church, and who think that the ministry of evil men is not useful and is ineffective.

ARTICLE IX
Baptism

———

Note: The Bible teaches that Baptism is a gift of God's grace by which He applies the benefits of Christ's life, death, and resurrection to us personally. Because all people are conceived and born in sin, we all need salvation. Because Baptism is God's way of bringing us salvation, infants should also be baptized. During the Reformation, as now, some Christian groups turned Baptism from God's saving activity into an act of Christian obedience. This view of Baptism arises from the denial of original sin and a semi-Pelagian view of salvation, whereby faith becomes the good work we contribute. This article concentrates on what God gives in this Sacrament.

———

1   Concerning Baptism, our churches teach that Baptism is necessary for salvation [Mark 16:16] and that God's grace is offered
2 through Baptism [Titus 3:4–7]. They teach that children are to be baptized [Acts 2:38–39]. Being offered to God through Baptism, they are received into God's grace.
3   Our churches condemn the Anabaptists, who reject the Baptism of children, and say that children are saved without Baptism.

ARTICLE X
The Lord's Supper

———

Note: By the time the Augsburg Confession was written, deep divisions had arisen among the various reformers concerning the Lord's Supper. The Lutherans were very careful to distance themselves from those who reject that the body and blood of Christ are in fact truly present in His Supper and distributed to all those who eat and drink. Transubstantiation, consubstantiation, or any other human speculation asks the wrong

question: *how* is Christ present? Lutheranism has no theory or philosophical explanation of how Christ is present. Rather, Lutherans insist on answering the *what* of the Lord's Supper. We believe, teach, and confess that of the bread, Christ said, "This is My body," and of the wine, "This is My blood." These are given and shed "for the forgiveness of sins" (Matthew 26:26–28). We reject any teaching that is contrary to our Lord's Word.

———

1   Our churches teach that the body and blood of Christ are truly present and distributed to those who eat the Lord's Supper [1 Corinthians 10:16]. They reject those who
2 teach otherwise.

ARTICLE XI
Confession

———

Note: By the time of the Reformation, the practice of confessing sins privately and confidentially to a pastor had been a well-accepted church practice for more than a thousand years. Private Confession and Absolution was never something Lutherans wanted to get rid of. As time went on, the practice fell into disuse, but clearly Article XI assumes that private Confession and Absolution will take place in the Lutheran Church. The problem addressed by this article is that the Roman Church demanded every sin be recalled and confessed. Clearly, this is humanly impossible and makes our forgiveness dependent on our work. Such teaching is certainly dangerous to repentant consciences, which need firm assurance that Christ forgives all sin.

———

1   Our churches teach that private Absolution should be retained in the churches, although listing all sins is not necessary for Confession. For, according to the Psalm, it
2 is impossible. "Who can discern his errors?" (Psalm 19:12).

IOANNES OECOLAMPADIVS
Basiliensis Ecclesiæ Pastor.

John Oecolampadius (1482–1531)

Ally of Zwingli who opposed Luther at the
Marburg Colloquy (1529). Condemned in
Article X of the Augsburg Confession.

ANNO AETATIS EIVS XLVIIL

Ulrich Zwingli (1484–1531)

Leader of the "Sacramentarians." The
Romanists tried to lump all Protestants
together. The Augsburg Confession was
clear that Lutherans rejected the teachings of Zwingli and others like him. After
Zwingli died in battle, John Calvin contin-
ued Zwingli's work, creating the Reformed
churches.

ARTICLE XII

Repentance

———

Note: The Roman teaching about repentance was the spark that ignited the Lutheran Reformation. When Luther learned his congregational members were buying indulgences, hoping to avert God's punishment for sins by paying money, he was incensed. Repentance is not about "paying off" God or making some satisfaction for our sin. Repentance is recognizing the reality of our sin and turning to God in faith for His mercy. God reveals our sin through His Law; He forgives our sin and restores us to a right relationship with Himself through His Gospel. While we affirm there is fruit of repentance, the focus of the Gospel must be clear: our sins are forgiven only because of Christ. Our lives in Christ are lives of repentance, returning again and again to the fount and source of all mercy, our Savior. Notice that this article rejects any teaching that implies our works of satisfaction are part of true repentance. Article XII strikes a fatal blow at the very heart of the Roman sacramental system.

———

Selling Indulgences

The pope (center) hands a commission to sell indulgences to a monk. Right: The purchase of an indulgence, with people being directed where to put their money. Left: A lame man asks for help, while others purchase their indulgences. Their names are being written on the indulgence receipt.

1 Our churches teach that there is forgiveness of sins for those who have fallen after
2 Baptism whenever they are converted. The Church ought to impart Absolution to those who return to repentance [Jeremiah 3:12].
3 Now, strictly speaking, repentance consists
4 of two parts. One part is contrition, that is, terrors striking the conscience through the
5 knowledge of sin. The other part is faith, which is born of the Gospel [Romans 10:17] or the Absolution and believes that for Christ's sake, sins are forgiven. It comforts the conscience and delivers it from ter-
6 ror. Then good works are bound to follow, which are the fruit of repentance [Galatians 5:22–23].
7 Our churches condemn the Anabaptists, who deny that those who have once been
8 justified can lose the Holy Spirit. They also condemn those who argue that some may reach such a state of perfection in this life that they cannot sin.
9 The Novatians also are condemned, who would not absolve those who had fallen after Baptism, though they returned to repentance.
10 Our churches also reject those who do not teach that forgiveness of sins comes through faith, but command us to merit grace through satisfactions of our own.

They also reject those who teach that it is necessary to perform works of satisfaction, commanded by Church law, in order to remit eternal punishment or the punishment of purgatory.

ARTICLE XIII
The Use of the Sacraments

———

Note: God gives the Sacraments to His people for their forgiveness, life, and salvation, and this happens as they call forth trust and confidence in Christ, the Savior. By the sixteenth century, the Roman Church had developed a complicated sacramental system that had transformed the Sacraments into meritorious works performed by priests. This was especially evident in the Mass, where priests "sacrificed" Christ again and again on behalf of the living and the dead. The Bible, however, reveals the key to the Sacraments: the promises of God. God attaches His Word of promise to the element of the Sacrament—water, wine, or bread—and gives and strengthens the faith of those receiving them.

———

1 Our churches teach that the Sacraments were ordained, not only to be marks of profession among men, but even more, to be signs and testimonies of God's will toward
2 us. They were instituted to awaken and confirm faith in those who use them. Therefore, we must use the Sacraments in such a way that faith, which believes the promises offered and set forth through the Sacraments, is increased [2 Thessalonians 1:3].
3 Therefore, they condemn those who teach that the Sacraments justify simply by the act of doing them. They condemn those who do not teach that faith, which believes that sins are forgiven, is required in the use of the Sacraments.

ARTICLE XIV
Order in the Church

———

Note: When this article speaks of a rightly ordered call, it refers to the Church's historic practice of placing personally and theologically qualified men into the office of preaching and teaching the Gospel and administering the Sacraments. No one in the Church can take such authority for himself or bestow such authority on his own. The ministry is conferred by means of a formal, public, and official call from the Church.

At the time this article was presented, it was understood that a minister's first call is publicly ratified and confirmed by means of prayer and the laying on of hands, ordination, a practice that dates back to the time of the apostles. In the Lutheran Confessions, "ordination" is a term often used as shorthand for both the call and ordination.

———

Our churches teach that no one should publicly teach in the Church, or administer the Sacraments, without a rightly ordered call.

ARTICLE XV
Church Ceremonies

———

Note: Lutheranism embraces the good historic traditions of the Church, especially those of the Western Church. These include such things as following the pattern of the Church year, lectionary readings from the Bible, a liturgical order of worship, various festival days, vestments worn by clergy, and the use of candles, crucifixes, and other objects. As this article makes very clear, in the Lutheran Church, rites, decorations, or traditions are never used or followed to appease God's wrath or to earn the forgiveness of sins. Lutheranism removed from the Church useless and harmful traditions such as monastic vows and insisting on certain foods on certain days.

———

1   Our churches teach that ceremonies ought to be observed that may be observed without sin. Also, ceremonies and other practices that are profitable for tranquility and good order in the Church (in particular, holy days, festivals, and the like) ought to be observed.

Yet, the people are taught that consciences are not to be burdened as though observing such things was necessary for salvation [Colossians 2:16–17]. They are also taught that human traditions instituted to make atonement with God, to merit grace, and to make satisfaction for sins are opposed to the Gospel and the doctrine of faith. So vows and traditions concerning meats and days, and so forth, instituted to merit grace and to make satisfaction for sins, are useless and contrary to the Gospel.

ARTICLE XVI
Civil Government

———

Note: It was important for Lutherans to make clear they did not share the beliefs of the radical reformers of the sixteenth century. Some of these radicals rejected all forms of order and authority, in both Church and State, even rejecting their homes and families in order to be "super spiritual." This article points to the biblical doctrine of the two kingdoms, a way of speaking about God's care for us spiritually though the Church and temporally through the various orders in society: chiefly, home and government. Christians live out their various callings in life in service to God and their fellow humans, doing so in the stations, or situations, to which God has called them.

———

Our churches teach that lawful civil regulations are good works of God. They teach that it is right for Christians to hold political office, to serve as judges, to judge matters by imperial laws and other existing laws, to impose just punishments, to engage in just wars, to serve as soldiers, to make legal contracts, to hold property, to take oaths when required by the magistrates, for a man to marry a wife, or a woman to be given in marriage [Romans 13; 1 Corinthians 7:2].

3   Our churches condemn the Anabaptists who forbid these political offices to Christians. 4 They also condemn those who do not locate evangelical perfection in the fear of God and in faith, but place it in forsaking 5 political offices. For the Gospel teaches an eternal righteousness of the heart (Romans 10:10). At the same time, it does not require the destruction of the civil state or the family. The Gospel very much requires that they be preserved as God's ordinances and that love be practiced in such ordinances. 6 Therefore, it is necessary for Christians to be 7 obedient to their rulers and laws. The only exception is when they are commanded to sin. Then they ought to obey God rather than men (Acts 5:29).

ARTICLE XVII
Christ's Return for Judgment

———∿∿———

Note: This article affirms the biblical view of the end times. It pointedly rejects any speculation or opinion about believers ruling the world before the final resurrection of the dead. It also rejects all theories about a "millennial" earthly rule of Christ as contrary to God's Word.

———∿∿———

1   Our churches teach that at the end of the world Christ will appear for judgment and will raise all the dead [1 Thessalonians 2 4:13–5:2]. He will give the godly and elect 3 eternal life and everlasting joys, but He will condemn ungodly people and the devils to be tormented without end [Matthew 25:31–46]. 4 Our churches condemn the Anabaptists, who think that there will be an end to the punishments of condemned men and devils. 5 Our churches also condemn those who

are spreading certain Jewish opinions, that before the resurrection of the dead the godly shall take possession of the kingdom of the world, the ungodly being everywhere suppressed.

ARTICLE XVIII
Free Will

———∿∿———

Note: By the time of the Reformation, the Roman Church had fully developed a false and potentially damning doctrine, one that stated that a person is able, to some degree, to strive for and receive God's mercy. Article XVIII asserts Scripture's teaching that people, apart from God's grace, are wholly incapable of perceiving spiritual things. The longest quote from a Church Father in the Augsburg Confession occurs here. It demonstrates Lutheranism's continuity with the Church catholic—in contrast to Roman error on this doctrine. Augustine echoes the Bible's teaching that while we humans can perform acts of civil righteousness, which may be called "good," spiritually we are evil and enemies of God. However, in Christ, our loving God breaks down the wall of hostility separating us from Him. By His Spirit, through His Word, He gives us Christ's perfect righteousness as a gift. In external, worldly matters we do have the freedom to make decisions according to human reason, but this does not mean, apart from God's grace, that we have similar powers in matters of eternal life.

———∿∿———

Our churches teach that a person's will 1 has some freedom to choose civil righteousness and to do things subject to reason. It has 2 no power, without the Holy Spirit, to work the righteousness of God, that is, spiritual righteousness. For "the natural person does not accept the things of the Spirit of God" (1 Corinthians 2:14). This righteousness is 3 worked in the heart when the Holy Spirit is received through the Word [Galatians 3:2–6].

4   This is what Augustine says in his *Hypognosticon*, Book III:

> We grant that all people have a free will. It is free as far as it has the judgment of reason. This does not mean that it is able, without God, either to begin, or at least to complete, anything that has to do with God. It is free only in works of this life,
> 5 whether good or evil. Good I call those works that spring from the good in nature, such as willing to labor in the field, to eat and drink, to have a friend, to clothe oneself, to build a house, to marry a wife, to raise cattle, to learn various useful arts, or whatsoever good applies to this life.
> 6 For all of these things depend on the providence of God. They are from
> 7 Him and exist through Him. Works that are willing to worship an idol, to commit murder, and so forth, I call evil.

8   Our churches condemn the Pelagians and others who teach that without the Holy Spirit, by natural power alone, we are able to love God above all things and do God's
9 commandments according to the letter. Although nature is able in a certain way to do the outward work (for it is able to keep the hands from theft and murder), yet it cannot produce the inward motions, such as the fear of God, trust in God, chastity, patience, and so on.

ARTICLE XIX
The Cause of Sin

Note: The blame for sin rests solely with the devil and with us, not with God. Apart from God's mercy in Christ, there is no hope for the wicked. Years after the Augsburg Confession was written, in order to accentuate the depth of mankind's sinful condition, some Lutherans would imply that sin is of the very essence of people. The result of this faulty teaching is that God becomes responsible for, indeed the Creator of, sin. Sin is a deep corruption of that which God created, and is entirely mankind's fault.

Our churches teach that although God creates and preserves nature, the cause of sin is located in the will of the wicked, that is, the devil and ungodly people. Without God's help, this will turns itself away from God, as Christ says, "When he lies, he speaks out of his own character" (John 8:44).

ARTICLE XX
Good Works

Note: This is another key article in the Augsburg Confession. Article XX offers more details about faith and works than what was previously written. Lutherans insist on the biblical truth that our good works do not save us. So they are sometimes accused of opposing good works. This article sets forth the Bible's clear teaching that good works are the fruit of faith, not the cause of our salvation. The Lutheran hymn "Salvation unto Us Has Come" offers a short, powerful summary of these essential Gospel truths:

> Faith clings to Jesus' cross alone
> And rests in Him unceasing;
> And by its fruits true faith is known,
> with love and hope increasing.
> For faith alone can justify;
> Works serve our neighbor and supply
> The proof that faith is living.

> (Paul Speratus, 1484–1531; tr.
> *The Lutheran Hymnal*, 1941, alt.)

Rome continues to insist that people are saved by God's grace, but not through faith alone. This teaching dangerously encourages people to believe they are able, even in some small way, to contribute toward their salvation. This diverts their focus from Christ and His merits to their own works. It also leads to despair, doubt, and uncertainty when people come to realize the enormity of their sin and wonder if in fact they have done "enough" to merit or deserve God's favor. After setting forth the proper biblical distinction between faith and good works, the Augsburg Confession asserts very clearly that our good works are necessary, not to merit grace, but because this is God's will for our lives. God's gift of saving faith enables us to do good works.

---

1 Our teachers are falsely accused of for-
2 bidding good works. Their published writings on the Ten Commandments, and other similar writings, bear witness that they have usefully taught about all estates and duties of life. They have taught well what is pleasing to God in every station and vocation in
3 life. Before now, preachers taught very little about these things. They encouraged only childish and needless works, such as particular holy days, particular fasts, brotherhoods, pilgrimages, services in honor of the saints, the use of rosaries, monasticism, and such
4 things. Since our adversaries have been admonished about these things, they are now unlearning them. They do not preach these unhelpful works as much as they used to.
5 In the past, there was only stunning silence about faith, but now they are beginning to
6 mention it. They do not teach that we are justified only by works. They join faith and works together, and say that we are justified
7 by faith and works. This teaching is more tolerable than the former one. It can offer more consolation than their old teaching.

The doctrine about faith, which ought to 8 be the chief doctrine in the Church, has remained unknown for so long. Everyone has to admit that there was the deepest silence in their sermons concerning the righteousness of faith. They only taught about works in the churches. This is why our teachers teach the churches about faith in this way.

First, they teach that our works cannot 9 reconcile God to us or merit forgiveness of sins, grace, and justification. We obtain reconciliation only by faith when we believe that we are received into favor for Christ's sake. He alone has been set forth as the Mediator and Atoning Sacrifice (1 Timothy 2:5), in order that the Father may be reconciled through Him. Therefore, whoever be- 10 lieves that he merits grace by works despises the merit and grace of Christ [Galatians 5:4]. In so doing, he is seeking a way to God without Christ, by human strength, although Christ Himself said, "I am the way, and the truth, and the life" (John 14:6).

This doctrine about faith is presented 11 everywhere by Paul, "By grace you have been saved through faith. And this is not your own doing; it is the gift of God" (Ephesians 2:8).

If anyone wants to be tricky and say that 12 we have invented a new interpretation of Paul, this entire matter is supported by the testimony of the Fathers. Augustine defends 13 grace and the righteousness of faith in many volumes against the merits of works. Am- 14 brose, in his book *The Calling of the Gentiles*, and elsewhere, teaches the same thing. In *The Calling of the Gentiles* he says,

> Redemption by Christ's blood would be worth very little, and God's mercy would not surpass man's works, if justification, which is accomplished through grace, were due to prior merits. So justification would not be

the free gift from a donor, but the reward due the laborer.

15   Spiritually inexperienced people despise this teaching. However, God-fearing and anxious consciences find by experience that it brings the greatest consolation. Consciences cannot be set at rest through any works, but only by faith, when they take the sure ground that for Christ's sake they have 16 a gracious God. As Paul teaches, "since we have been justified by faith, we have peace 17 with God" (Romans 5:1). This whole doctrine must be related to the conflict of the terrified conscience. It cannot be understood 18 apart from that conflict. Therefore, inexperienced and irreverent people have poor judgment in this matter because they dream that Christian righteousness is nothing but civil and philosophical righteousness.

19   Until now consciences were plagued with the doctrine of works. They did not 20 hear consolation from the Gospel. Some people were driven by conscience into the desert and into monasteries, hoping to 21 merit grace by a monastic life. Some people came up with other works to merit grace 22 and make satisfaction for sins. That is why the need was so great for teaching and renewing the doctrine of faith in Christ, so that anxious consciences would not be without consolation but would know that grace, forgiveness of sins, and justification are received by faith in Christ.

23   People are also warned that the term *faith* does not mean simply a knowledge of a history, such as the ungodly and devil have [James 2:19]. Rather, it means a faith that believes, not merely the history, but also the effect of the history. In other words, it believes this article: the forgiveness of sins. We have grace, righteousness, and forgiveness of sins through Christ.

24   The person who knows that he has a Father who is gracious to him through Christ truly knows God [John 14:7]. He also knows that God cares for him [1 Peter 5:7], and he calls upon God [Romans 10:13]. In a word, he is not without God, as are the heathen. 25 For devils and the ungodly are not able to believe this article: the forgiveness of sins. Hence, they hate God as an enemy [Romans 8:7] and do not call Him [Romans 3:11–12] 26 and expect no good from Him. Augustine also warns his readers about the word *faith* and teaches that the term is used in the Scriptures, not for the knowledge that is in the ungodly, but for the confidence that consoles and encourages the terrified mind.

27   Furthermore, we teach that it is necessary to do good works. This does not mean that we merit grace by doing good works, but because it is God's will [Ephesians 2:10]. 28 It is only by faith, and nothing else, that 29 forgiveness of sins is apprehended. The Holy Spirit is received through faith, hearts are renewed and given new affections, and then they are able to bring forth good works. 30 Ambrose says: "Faith is the mother of a good will and doing what is right." Without 31 the Holy Spirit people are full of ungodly desires. They are too weak to do works that are good in God's sight [John 15:5]. Besides, 32 they are in the power of the devil, who pushes human beings into various sins, ungodly opinions, and open crimes. We see this in 33 the philosophers, who, although they tried to live an honest life could not succeed, but were defiled with many open crimes. Such 34 is human weakness, without faith and without the Holy Spirit, when governed only by human strength.

35   Therefore, it is easy to see that this doctrine is not to be accused of banning good works. Instead, it is to be commended all the more because it shows how we are enabled

36 to do good works. For without faith, human nature cannot, in any way, do the works of the First or Second Commandment [1 Cor-

37 inthians 2:14]. Without faith, human nature does not call upon God, nor expect anything from Him, nor bear the cross [Matthew 16:24]. Instead, human nature seeks and

38 trusts in human help. So when there is no faith and trust in God, all kinds of lusts and human intentions rule in the heart [Genesis

39 6:5]. This is why Christ says, "Apart from Me you can do nothing" (John 15:5). That is

40 why the Church sings: "Lacking Your divine favor, there is nothing in man. Nothing in him is harmless."

ARTICLE XXI
Worship of the Saints

———

Note: The Early Church had developed an appreciation for those who confessed, and sometimes died for, their faith. However, deep corruption had developed within the Church regarding the honor given to the saints, resulting in what could only be described as idolatrous worship. Those who have gone before us in the faith are to be honored, remembered, and imitated according to our various stations and callings in life. That is clear. However, it is clearly contrary to Scripture to teach that the saints are to be prayed to and invoked for aid. There is simply no command, no example, and no promise in Scripture indicating that we should pray to our departed brothers and sisters in Christ.

———

1   Our churches teach that the history of saints may be set before us so that we may follow the example of their faith and good works, according to our calling. For example, the emperor may follow the example of David [2 Samuel] in making war to drive away the Turk from his country. For both

2 are kings. But the Scriptures do not teach that we are to call on the saints or to ask the saints for help. Scripture sets before us the one Christ as the Mediator, Atoning Sacrifice, High Priest, and Intercessor [1 Timothy 2:5–6]. He is to be prayed to. He

3 has promised that He will hear our prayer [John 14:13]. This is the worship that He approves above all other worship, that He be called upon in all afflictions. "If anyone does

4 sin, we have an advocate with the Father" (1 John 2:1).

[A Summary Statement]

1   This then is nearly a complete summary of our teaching. As can be seen, there is nothing that varies from the Scriptures, or from the Church universal, or from the Church of Rome, as known from its writers. Since this is the case, those who insist that our teachers are to be regarded

2 as heretics are judging harshly. There is, however, disagreement on certain abuses that have crept into the Church without rightful authority. Even here, if there are some differences, the bishops should bear with us patiently because of the Confession we have just reviewed. Even the Church's canon law is not so severe that it demands the same rites everywhere. Nor, for that

3 matter, have the rites of all churches ever been the same. Although, in large part, the

4 ancient rites are diligently observed among us. It is a false and hate-filled charge that our churches have abolished all the ceremonies instituted in ancient times. But the

5 abuses connected with the ordinary rites have been a common source of complaint. They have been corrected to some extent since they could not be approved with a good conscience.

A Review of the Various Abuses That Have Been Corrected

1   Our churches do not dissent from any article of the faith held by the Church catholic. They only omit some of the newer abuses. They have been erroneously accepted through the corruption of the times, contrary to the intent of canon law. Therefore, we pray that Your Imperial Majesty will graciously hear what has been changed and why the people are not compelled to observe those things that are abuses against their
2 conscience. Your Imperial Majesty should not believe those who have tried to stir up hatred against us by spreading strange lies
3 among the people. They have given rise to this controversy by stirring up the minds of good people. Now they are trying to increase the controversy using the same methods.
4 Your Imperial Majesty will undoubtedly find that the form of doctrine and ceremonies among us are not as intolerable as these
5 ungodly and ill-intentioned men claim. Besides, the truth cannot be gathered from common rumors or the attacks of enemies.
6 It can easily be judged that if the churches observed ceremonies correctly, their dignity would be maintained and reverence and piety would increase among the people.

ARTICLE XXII

Both Kinds in the Sacrament

———

Note: Prior to the Reformation, the practice had developed of withholding the consecrated wine from the laity during the Lord's Supper. Only the consecrated bread was distributed to them. However, priests who celebrated Mass drank from the cup. Theories developed within the Church to help support this practice. One stated that the bread alone was enough for the laity, since Christ's body must also contain His blood.

The practice of withholding the cup from the congregation was clearly contrary to Scripture and was an insult to God's royal priests—all those who trust in Christ for the forgiveness of sins. The Early Church Fathers spoke about *all* of God's people receiving both "kinds," or elements, of this Holy Meal.

———

The laity are given both kinds in the 1 Sacrament of the Lord's Supper because this practice has the Lord's command, "Drink of it, all of you" (Matthew 26:27). Christ has 2 clearly commanded that all should drink from the cup.

And lest anyone misleadingly say that 3 this refers only to priests, in 1 Corinthians 11:27 Paul cites an example. From this it appears that the whole congregation used both kinds. This practice has remained in 4 the Church for a long time. It is not known when, or by whom, or by whose authority, it was changed. Cardinal Cusanus mentions the time when it was approved. Cyprian in 5 some places testifies that the blood was given to the people. Jerome testifies to the same 6 thing when he says, "The priests administer the Eucharist and distribute the blood of Christ to the people." Indeed, Pope Gelasius 7 commands that the Sacrament not be divided (dist. II., *De Consecratione, cap. Comperimus*). Only a recent custom has changed this. 8

It is clear that any custom introduced 9 against God's commandments is not to be allowed, as Church law bears witness (dist. III., *cap. Veritate*, and the following chapters). This custom has been received, not only 10 against the Scripture, but also against old canon law and the example of the Church. Therefore, if anyone preferred to use both 11 kinds in the Sacrament, they should not have been compelled to do otherwise, as an offense against their conscience. Because 12 the division of the Sacrament does not agree with the ordinance of Christ, it is our custom to omit the procession [with the host], which has been used before.

ARTICLE XXIII
The Marriage of Priests

———

Note: Underlying the issue of forced priestly celibacy, as with other abuses arising in the Church, is the authority of the Church to command and forbid something not mentioned in Scripture. The Lutherans maintained that the Church has no authority from God to command what He has not commanded, nor to forbid what He has not forbidden. The Bible clearly teaches that the apostle Peter had a wife. This example should have served as convincing proof that priestly marriages were God pleasing. That there are men who are given the gift of chastity is affirmed, but the view that the Church can, and should, forbid all who wish to be priests from marrying is resoundingly rejected. Marriage is a gift from God to be received with thanksgiving both by laypeople and clergy. To suggest otherwise is to introduce a teaching of the evil one into the Church.

———

1 Complaints about unchaste priests are
2 common. Platina writes that it is for this reason that Pope Pius is reported to have said that although there are reasons why marriage was taken away from priests, there are far more important reasons why it should be
3 given back. Since our priests wanted to avoid these open scandals, they married wives and taught that it was lawful for them to enter
4 into marriage. First, because Paul says, "Because of the temptation to sexual immorality, each man should have his own wife" and "It is better to marry than to be aflame with passion" (1 Corinthians 7:2, 9b).
5 Second, Christ says, "Not everyone can receive this saying" (Matthew 19:11), where

He teaches that not everyone is able to lead a single life. God created human beings for procreation (Genesis 1:28). It is not within a 6 person's power, without God giving a unique gift, to change this creation. ‹For it is clear, as many have confessed, that no good, honest, chaste life, no Christian, sincere, upright conduct has resulted from the attempt to lead a single life. Instead, a horrible, fearful unrest and torment of conscience has been felt by many until the end.› Therefore, those 7 who are not able to lead a single life ought to marry. No human law, no vow, can destroy 8 God's commandment and ordinance. For 9 these reasons the priests teach that it is lawful for them to marry wives.

It is clear that in the Ancient Church 10 priests were married men. For Paul says, 11 "An overseer must be the husband of one wife" (1 Timothy 3:2). Four hundred years 12 ago in Germany, for the first time, priests were violently forced to lead a single life. They offered such resistance that when the archbishop of Mainz was about to publish the pope's decree about celibacy, he was almost killed in a riot by enraged priests. This 13 matter was handled so harshly that not only was marriage forbidden in the future, but existing marriages were torn apart, contrary to all laws, both divine and human. This was even contrary to canon law itself, as made by not only popes, but also by the most celebrated synods.

Seeing that man's nature is gradually 14 growing weaker as the world grows older, it is good to be on guard to make sure no more vices work their way into Germany.

Furthermore, God ordained marriage to 15 be a help against human weakness. Canon 16 law itself says that the old rigor ought to be relaxed now and then, in these latter times, because of human weakness. We wish this would also be done in this matter. We expect 17 that at some point churches will lack pastors if marriage continues to be forbidden.

18   While God's commandment is in force, and the custom of the Church is well known, impure celibacy will cause many scandals, adulteries, and other crimes that deserve punishment from just rulers. In light of all this, it is incredibly cruel that the mar-

19   riage of priests is forbidden. God has com-

20   manded that marriage be honored. Marriage is most highly honored in the laws of all well-ordered commonwealths, even among

21   the heathen. But now men, even priests, are cruelly put to death, contrary to the intent of canon law, for no other reason than that they

22   are married. Paul, in 1 Timothy 4, says that a doctrine of demons forbids marriage (vv.

23   1–3). This is clearly seen by how laws against marriage are enforced with such penalties.

24   Since no human law can destroy God's command, neither can it be done by any

25   vow. So Cyprian advises women who do not keep the promise they made to remain chaste, that they should marry. He says (Book I, Epistle XI), "If they are unwilling or unable to persevere, it is better for them to marry than to fall into the fire by their lusts. They should certainly give no offense to their

26   brothers and sisters." And even canon law shows some leniency toward those who have taken vows before the proper age, as has been the case up to this point.

ARTICLE XXIV

The Mass

———

Note: This article clearly demonstrates Lutheranism's desire to continue—not to reject—the wholesome, beneficial, and historic worship practices of the Church. Lutheranism retained the traditional form of the Mass, that is, the service of Holy Communion. In many respects, the ceremonies and liturgy of the Lutheran Church were very similar to those of the Roman Church. The difference lay in Lutheranism's rejection of false teaching concerning the Mass: that somehow, and without faith, simply by attending and observing the spectacle of the Mass, people could merit the forgiveness of sins. Worst of all was Rome's teaching that a priest saying Mass is actually offering Christ in an unbloody manner to appease God and secure His favor. Masses became a source of considerable revenue for the Church, since people were encouraged to "sponsor" the saying of a Mass for their living—and dead—friends and relatives. All this is entirely contrary to Christ's institution of the Lord's Supper. He gave the Church this Sacrament as a gift and blessing, to be used in faith by the people of God.

———

1   Our churches are falsely accused of abolishing the Mass. The Mass is held among us and celebrated with the highest reverence.

2   Nearly all the usual ceremonies are also preserved, except that the parts sung in Latin are interspersed here and there with German hymns. These have been added to teach the

3   people. For ceremonies are needed for this reason alone, that the uneducated be taught ‹what they need to know about Christ›. Not

4   only has Paul commanded that a language understood by the people be used in church (1 Corinthians 14:2, 9), but human law has

5   also commanded it. All those able to do so partake of the Sacrament together. This also increases the reverence and devotion of

6   public worship. No one is admitted to the

7   Sacrament without first being examined. The people are also advised about the dignity and use of the Sacrament, about how it brings great consolation to anxious consciences, so that they too may learn to believe God and to expect and ask from Him all that is

8   good. This worship pleases God [Colossians

9 1:9–10]. Such use of the Sacrament nourishes true devotion toward God. Therefore, it does not appear that the Mass is more devoutly celebrated among our adversaries than among us.

10 It is clear that for a long time the most public and serious complaint among all good people is that the Mass has been made base and profane by using it to gain filthy wealth [1 Timothy 3:3]. 11 Everyone knows how great this abuse is in all the churches. They know what sort of men say Masses for a fee or an income, and how many celebrate 12 these Masses contrary to canon law. Paul severely threatens those who use the Eucharist in an unworthy manner, "Whoever eats the bread or drinks the cup of the Lord in an unworthy manner will be guilty of profaning the body and blood of the Lord" (1 Corinthians 11:27). 13 Therefore, when our priests were warned about this sin, private Masses were discontinued among us, since hardly any private Masses were celebrated except for the sake of filthy gain.

14 The bishops were not ignorant of these abuses. If they had corrected them in time, 15 there would now be less discord. But until now they have been responsible for many 16 corruptions seeping into the Church. Now, when it is too late, they begin to complain about the Church's troubles. This disturbance has been caused simply by those abuses that were so open that they could no 17 longer be tolerated. There have been great disagreements about the Mass, that is, the 18 Sacrament. Perhaps the world is being punished for profaning the Mass for such a long time and for tolerating this in the churches for so many centuries by the very men who were both able and duty-bound 19 to correct this situation. It is written in the Ten Commandments, "The LORD will not hold him guiltless who takes His name in vain" (Exodus 20:7). 20 But since the world began, nothing that God ever ordained seems to have been so abused for filthy wealth as the Mass.

21 An opinion was added that infinitely increased private Masses. It states that Christ, by His passion, made satisfaction for original sin and instituted the Mass as an offering for daily sins, both venial and mortal. 22 From this opinion has arisen the common belief that the Mass takes away the sins of the living and the dead simply by performing the outward act. 23 Then they began to argue about whether one Mass said for many is worth as much as special Masses for individuals. This resulted in an infinite number of Masses. ⟨With this work, people wanted to obtain from God all that they needed, and in the meantime, trust in Christ and true worship were forgotten⟩.

24 Our teachers have warned that these opinions depart from the Holy Scripture and diminish the glory of the passion of Christ. 25 For Christ's passion was an offering and satisfaction, not only for original guilt, but also for all other sins, as it is written, 26 "We have been sanctified through the offering of the body of Jesus Christ once for all" (Hebrews 10:10). 27 Also, "By a single offering He has perfected for all time those who are being sanctified" (Hebrews 10:14). ⟨It is an unheard-of innovation in the Church to teach that by His death Christ has made satisfaction only for original sin and not for all other sin. So it is hoped that everybody will understand that this error has been rebuked for good reason.⟩

28 Scripture teaches that we are justified before God, through faith in Christ, when we believe that our sins are forgiven for Christ's sake. 29 Now if the Mass takes away the sins of the living and the dead simply by performing it, justification comes by doing

Masses, and not of faith. Scripture does not allow this.

30   But Christ commands us, "Do this in remembrance of Me" (Luke 22:19). Therefore, the Mass was instituted so that those who use the Sacrament should remember, in faith, the benefits they receive through Christ and how their anxious consciences 31 are cheered and comforted. To remember Christ is to remember His benefits. It means to realize that they are truly offered 32 to us. It is not enough only to remember 33 history. (The Jewish people and the ungodly also remember this.) Therefore, the Mass is to be used for administering the Sacrament to those who need consolation. Ambrose says, "Because I always sin, I always need to take the medicine."

34   Because the Mass is for the purpose of giving the Sacrament, we have Communion every holy day, and if anyone desires the Sacrament, we also offer it on other days, when it is given to all who ask for it. This custom 35 is not new in the Church. The Fathers before Gregory make no mention of any private Mass, but they speak a lot about the common 36 Mass, ‹Communion›. Chrysostom says "that the priest stands daily at the altar, inviting some to the Communion and keeping back 37 others." It appears from the ancient council decisions that one person celebrated the Mass from whom all the other presbyters and deacons received the body of the Lord. 38 The records of the decisions of the Council of Nicaea state, "Let the deacons, according to their order, receive the Holy Communion after the presbyters, from the bishop or from 39 a presbyter." Paul, in 1 Corinthians 11:33, has this command in regard to Communion: "wait for one another" so that there may be a common participation.

Therefore, since the Mass among us fol- 40 lows the example of the Church, taken from the Scripture and the Fathers, we are confident that it cannot be disapproved. This is especially so because we keep the public ceremonies, which are for the most part similar to those previously in use. Only the number of Masses differs. Without a doubt, these might be reduced in a helpful way, because of very great and clear abuses. For 41 in older times, even in churches attended the most often, the Mass was not celebrated every day, as the *Tripartite History* (Book 9, chap. 33) testifies, "In Alexandria, every Wednesday and Friday the Scriptures are read, and the doctors expound them, and all things are done, except the solemn rite of Communion."

ARTICLE XXV

Confession

—∾∾—

Note: The practice of private Confession and Absolution with one's pastor has fallen out of use in many Lutheran congregations. This was never Luther's intention. Neither was private Confession and Absolution abandoned during the first two centuries of Lutheran history. What the Lutheran Reformation corrected were the false teachings about Confession. Problems arose in the Church when teachings about Confession made "satisfactions" such a prominent part of it. When people were told to do certain activities (e.g., repeating the Hail Mary or doing acts of contrition) to "make up" for their sins, Christ's Gospel was overshadowed, if not completely hidden. Lutheranism, therefore, did away with the antibiblical teaching about satisfaction for sins and the requirement that people try to remember and confess each sin committed.

—∾∾—

1   Confession in the churches is not abolished among us. The body of the Lord is not usually given to those who have not been examined [1 Corinthians 11:27–28]

2   and absolved. The people are very carefully taught about faith in the Absolution.

3   Before, there was profound silence about faith. Our people are taught that they should highly prize the Absolution as being God's

4   voice and pronounced by God's command. The Power of the Keys [Matthew 16:19] is set forth in its beauty. They are reminded what great consolation it brings to anxious consciences and that God requires faith to believe such Absolution as a voice sounding from heaven [e.g., John 12:28–30]. They are taught that such faith in Christ truly obtains

5   and receives the forgiveness of sins. Before, satisfactions were praised without restraint, but little was said about faith, Christ's merit, and the righteousness of faith. Therefore, on this point, our churches are by no means

6   to be blamed. Even our adversaries have to concede the point that our teachers have diligently taught the doctrine of repentance and laid it open.

7   Our churches teach that naming every sin is not necessary and that consciences should not be burdened with worry about naming every sin. It is impossible to recount all sins, as Psalm 19:12 testifies: "Who can

8   discern his errors?" Also Jeremiah 17:9, "The heart is deceitful above all things, and desperately sick; who can understand it?"

9   If only sins that can be named are forgiven, consciences could never find peace. For many sins cannot be seen or remembered.

10   The ancient writers also testify that a listing

11   of sins is not necessary. For in the Decrees, Chrysostom is quoted. He says,

> I do not say that you should make your sins known in public, nor that you should accuse yourself before others, but I would have you obey the prophet who says, "Make known your ways before God" [Psalm 37:5]. Therefore, confess your sins before God, the true Judge, with prayer. Tell your errors, not with the tongue, but with the memory of your conscience, and so forth.

12   And the Gloss (*Of Repentance*, Distinct. V, *Cap. Consideret*) admits that Confession is of human right only. Nevertheless,

13   because of the great benefit of Absolution, and because it is otherwise useful to the conscience, Confession is retained among us.

ARTICLE XXVI

The Distinction of Meats

———

Note: Choosing not to eat particular foods, or any food at all, at particular times or on particular occasions is entirely a matter of Christian freedom. By the time of the Reformation, however, the Church had devised complex regulations commanding abstinence from certain foods on certain days. Church teaching misled people into believing that by following such regulations they merited God's grace and favor. Such a theory is entirely contrary to the Gospel, overturns the all-sufficient merit of Jesus Christ, and replaces Him with human works. Contrived laws such as these placed enormous burdens on the common people, who frequently considered themselves less spiritual than the monks and nuns who adhered to these dietary regulations very closely. Bodily discipline and working to curb one's sinful desires is entirely appropriate and necessary, but never is it to be suggested that such activities earn God's grace. In highlighting the issue of dietary restrictions, the Augsburg Confession once more repeats that Lutherans do not do away with good traditions and practices, such as the order of Bible readings in the Communion Service, but only such things as take away from the Gospel.

———∿∿∿———

1   Not only the people, but also those teaching in the churches, have generally been persuaded to believe in making distinctions between meats, and similar human traditions. They believe these are useful works for meriting grace and are able to make sat-
2   isfaction for sins. From this there developed the view that new ceremonies, new orders, new holy days, and new fastings were instituted daily. Teachers in the Church required these works as a necessary service to merit grace. They greatly terrified people's consciences when they left any of these things
3   out. Because of this viewpoint, the Church has suffered great damage.
4   First, the chief part of the Gospel—the doctrine of grace and of the righteousness of faith—has been obscured by this view. The Gospel should stand out as the most prominent teaching in the Church, in order that Christ's merit may be well known and faith, which believes that sins are forgiven for Christ's sake, be exalted far above works.
5   Therefore, Paul also lays the greatest stress on this article, putting aside the Law and human traditions, in order to show that Christian righteousness is something other than such works [Romans 14:17]. Christian righteousness is the faith that believes that
6   sins are freely forgiven for Christ's sake. But this doctrine of Paul has been almost completely smothered by traditions, which have produced the opinion that we must merit grace and righteousness by making distinc-
7   tions in meats and similar services. When repentance was taught, there was no mention made of faith. Only works of satisfaction were set forth. And so repentance seemed to stand entirely on these works.

8   Second, these traditions have hindered God's commandments, because traditions were placed far above God's commandments. Christianity was thought to stand wholly on the observance of certain holy days, rites, fasts, and vestments. These ob-
9   servances won the exalted title of the "spiritual life" and the "perfect life." Meanwhile,
10   God's commandments, according to each one's vocation, or calling, were without honor. These works include a father raising his children, a mother bearing children, a prince governing the commonwealth—these were considered to be worldly and thus imperfect works, far below the glittering observances of the Church. This error greatly
11   tormented people with devout consciences. They grieved that they were held in an imperfect state of life, as in marriage, in the office of ruler, or in other civil services. They admired the monks and others like them. They falsely thought that these people's observances were more acceptable to God.
12   Third, traditions brought great danger to consciences. It was impossible to keep all traditions, and yet people considered these observances to be necessary acts of worship. Gerson writes that many fell into despair,
13   and that some even took their own lives, because they felt that they were not able to satisfy the traditions. All the while, they had never heard about the consoling righteousness of faith and grace. We see that
14   the academics and theologians gather the traditions and seek ways to relieve and ease consciences. They do not free consciences enough, but sometimes entangle them even more! The schools and sermons have been
15   so occupied with gathering these "traditions" that they do not even have enough leisure time to touch on Scripture. They do not pursue the far more useful doctrine of faith, the cross, hope, the dignity of secular affairs,

16 and consolation for severely tested consciences. Therefore, Gerson and some other theologians have complained sadly that because of all this striving after traditions, they were prevented from giving attention to a

17 better kind of doctrine. Augustine forbids that people's consciences should be burdened. He prudently advises Januarius that he must know that they are to be observed as things neither commanded by God nor forbidden, for such are his words.

18 Therefore, our teachers must not be regarded as having taken up this matter rashly or from hatred of the bishops, as some falsely

19 suspect. There was a great need to warn the churches of these errors that arose from

20 misunderstanding the traditions. The Gospel compels us to insist on the doctrine of grace and the righteousness of faith in the churches. This cannot be understood if people think that they merit grace by observances of their own choice.

21 So our churches have taught that we cannot merit grace or be justified by observing human traditions. We must not think that such observances are necessary

22 acts of worship. Here we add testimonies of Scripture. Christ defends the apostles who had not observed the usual tradition (Matthew 15:3). This had to do with a matter that was not unlawful, but rather, neither commanded or forbidden. It was similar to the purifications of the Law. He said in Matthew 15:9, "In vain do they worship Me, teaching as doctrines the command-

23 ments of men." Therefore, He does not require a useless human service. Shortly after, He adds, "It is not what goes into the mouth that defiles a person, but what comes out of the mouth; this defiles a

24 person" (Matthew 15:11). So also Paul, in Romans 14:17, "The kingdom of God is not a matter of eating and drinking but

of righteousness and peace and joy in the

25 Holy Spirit," and in Colossians 2:16, "Let no one pass judgment on you in questions of food and drink, or with regard to . . . a Sabbath." And again, "If with Christ you

26 died to the elemental spirits of the world, why, as if you were still alive in the world, do you submit to regulations—'Do not handle, Do not taste, Do not touch'" [Colossians 2:20–21]. Peter says, "Why are you

27 putting God to the test by placing a yoke on the neck of the disciples that neither our fathers nor we have been able to bear? But we believe that we will be saved through the grace of the Lord Jesus, just as they will" (Acts 15:10–11). Here Peter forbids bur-

28 dening consciences with many rites, either from Moses or others. In 1 Timothy 4:1–3

29 Paul calls the prohibition of meats a teaching of demons. It is contrary to the Gospel to institute or do such works thinking that we merit grace through them, or as though Christianity could not exist without such service of God.

30 Our adversaries object by accusing our teachers of being against discipline and the subduing of the flesh. Just the opposite is true, as can be learned from our teachers'

31 writings. They have always taught that Christians are to bear the cross [Mat-

32 thew 16:24] by enduring afflictions. This is genuine and sincere subduing of the flesh [1 Peter 2:11], to be crucified with Christ

33 through various afflictions. Furthermore, they teach that every Christian ought to train and subdue himself with bodily restraints, or bodily exercises and labors. Then neither overindulgence nor laziness may tempt him to sin. But they do not teach that we may merit grace or make sat-

34 isfaction for sins by such exercises. Such outward discipline ought to be taught at all

35 times, not only on a few set days. Christ

36 commands, "Watch yourselves lest your hearts be weighed down with dissipation and drunkenness" (Luke 21:34). Also in Matthew 17:21, "This kind never comes
37 out except by prayer and fasting." Paul also says, "I discipline my body and keep it
38 under control" (1 Corinthians 9:27). Here he clearly shows that he was keeping his body under control, not to merit forgiveness of sins by that discipline, but to keep his body in subjection and prepared for spiritual things, for carrying out the duties of his call-
39 ing. Therefore, we do not condemn fasting in itself [Isaiah 58:3–7], but the traditions that require certain days and certain meats, with peril of conscience, as though such works were a necessary service.

40 Nevertheless, we keep many traditions that are leading to good order [1 Corinthians 14:40] in the Church, such as the order of Scripture lessons in the Mass and the
41 chief holy days. At the same time, we warn people that such observances do not justify us before God, and that it is not sinful if we omit such things, without causing of-
42 fense. The Fathers knew of such freedom in
43 human ceremonies. In the East they kept Easter at another time than at Rome. When the Romans accused the Eastern Church of schism, they were told by others that such practices do not need to be the same every-
44 where. Irenaeus says, "Diversity concerning fasting does not destroy the harmony of faith." Pope Gregory says, in Dist. XII, that such diversity does not violate the unity of
45 the Church. In the *Tripartite History*, Book 9, many examples of different rites are gathered, and the following statement is made:

> It was not the mind of the apostles to enact rules concerning holy days, but to preach godliness and a holy life.

ARTICLE XXVII
Monastic Vows

———

Note: This article has in view Martin Luther's experience in the monastery, along with what other former monks had to say about life in the cloister. The idea that a person should hide himself behind the walls of a monastery, and perform spiritual works to make himself more worthy of God's favor, has no biblical justification at all. During the Middle Ages, many common people believed that only priests, monks, or nuns were truly performing spiritual work. But such a view contradicts God's Word, which teaches how all of life is an opportunity to serve God—giving Him glory by serving our neighbor. Even today, it is assumed that activities at church are somehow of greater value than the common, everyday duties life requires of us. This article extols such biblical duties as being a faithful husband, wife, son, or daughter, and takes great care to reject monasticism and explain how harmful and dangerous it is for those who are entrapped in it. Forcing chastity on those who have not been given this gift is particularly harmful, since many are led to believe they merit God's grace by means of their sacrifice, not the sacrifice of Christ.

———

1 It will be easier to understand what we teach about monastic vows by considering the state of the monasteries and how many things were done every day contrary to
2 canon law. In Augustine's time they were free associations. Later, when discipline was corrupted, vows were added for the purpose of restoring discipline, as in a care-
3 fully planned prison. Gradually, many other regulations were added besides vows. These
4 binding rules were laid upon many before the lawful age, contrary to canon law.

5   Many entered monastic life through ignorance. They were not able to judge their own strength, though they were old enough. 6 They were trapped and compelled to remain, even though some could have been freed by the kind provision of canon law. 7 This was more the case in convents of women than of monks, although more consideration should have been shown the weaker sex [1 Peter 3:7]. 8 This rigor displeased many good people before this time, who saw that young men and women were thrown into convents for a living. They saw what unfortunate results came of this procedure, how it created scandals, and what snares were cast upon consciences! 9 They were sad that the authority of canon law in so great a matter was utterly set aside and despised. 10 In addition to all these evil things, a view of vows was added that displeased even the more considerate monks. They taught that monastic vows were equal to 11 Baptism. They taught that a monastic life merited forgiveness of sins and justification 12 before God. Yes, they even added that the monastic life not only merited righteousness before God, but even greater merit, since it was said that the monastic life not only kept God's basic law, but also the so-called "evangelical counsels."

13   So they made people believe that the profession of monasticism was far better than Baptism, and that the monastic life was more meritorious than that of rulers, pastors, and others, who serve in their calling according to God's commands, without any 14 man-made services. None of these things can be denied. This is all found in their own books about monasticism.

15   How did all this come about in monasteries? At one time they were schools of theology and other branches of learning, producing pastors and bishops for the benefit of the Church. Now it is another thing. It is needless to go over what everyone knows. Before, they came together for 16 the sake of learning, now they claim that monasticism is a lifestyle instituted to merit grace and righteousness. They even preach that it is a state of perfection! They put monasticism far above all other kinds of life ordained by God. 17 We have mentioned all these things without hateful exaggeration so that our teachers' doctrine on monasticism may be better understood.

First, concerning monks who marry, 18 our teachers say that it is lawful for anyone who is not suited for the single life to enter into marriage. Monastic vows cannot destroy what God has commanded and ordained. 19 God's commandment is this, "Because of the temptation to sexual immorality, each man should have his own wife" (1 Corinthians 7:2). 20 It is not just a command given by God. God has created and ordained marriage for those who are not given an exception to natural order by God's special work. This is what is taught according to the text in Genesis 2:18, "It is not good that the man should be alone." 21 Therefore, those who obey this command and ordinance of God do not sin.

What objection can be raised to this? Let 22 people praise the obligation of a monastic vow as much as they want, but they will never be able to destroy God's commandment by means of a monastic vow. 23 Canon law teaches that superiors can make exceptions to monastic vows; how much less are such monastic vows in force that are contrary to God's commandments!

If, in fact, an obligation to a monastic 24 vow could never be changed for any reason, the Roman popes could never have granted exceptions to the vows. For it is not lawful for someone to make an exception to what

George, Margrave of Brandenburg (1484–1543)

A courageous ally of John the Steadfast. Stood up to the emperor at the Diet of Augsburg, telling Charles he would sooner have his head cut off than deny Christ and His Word. Also called George the Pious.

25 is truly from God. The Roman pontiffs have wisely judged that mercy is to be observed in these monastic obligations. That is why we read that many times they have made special arrangements and exceptions with monastic

26 vows. The case of the King of Aragon, who was called back from the monastery, is well known, and there are also examples in our own times.

27   In the second place, why do our adversaries exaggerate the obligation or effect of a vow when, at the same time, they do not have anything to say about the nature of the vow itself? A vow should be something that is possible; it should be a decision that is made freely and after careful deliberation.

28 We all know how possible perpetual chastity

29 actually is in reality, and just how few people actually do take this vow freely and deliberately! Young women and men, before they are able to make their own decision about this, are persuaded, and sometimes even forced, to take the vow of chastity.

30 Therefore, it is not fair to insist so rigorously on the obligation. Everyone knows that taking a vow that is not made freely and deliberately is against the very nature of a true vow.

31   Most canonical laws overturn vows made before the age of fifteen. Before that age a person does not seem able to make a wise judgment and to decide to make a life-

32 long commitment like this. There is another canon law that adds even more years to this limit, showing that the vow of chastity should not be made before the age of eighteen. So which of these two canon laws should we fol-

33 low? Most people leaving the monastery have a valid excuse, since they took their vows before they were fifteen or eighteen.

Finally, even though it might be possible 34 to condemn a person who breaks a vow, it does not follow that it is right to dissolve such a person's marriage. Augustine denies 35 that they ought to be dissolved (XXVII. Quaest. I, Cap. *Nuptiarum*). Augustine's authority should not be taken lightly, even though some wish to do so today.

Although it appears that God's com- 36 mand about marriage delivers many from their vows, our teachers introduce another argument about vows to show that they are void. Every service of God, established and chosen by people to merit justification and grace, without God's commandment, is wicked. For Christ says in Matthew 15:9, "In vain do they worship Me, teaching as doctrines the commandments of men." Paul teaches everywhere that righteousness 37 is not to be sought in self-chosen practices and acts of worship, devised by people. Righteousness comes by faith to those who believe that they are received by God into grace for Christ's sake.

It is clear for all to see that the monks 38 have taught that services made up by people make satisfaction for sins and merit grace and justification. What else is this than detracting from Christ's glory and hiding and denying the righteousness that comes through faith? Therefore, it follows that 39 monastic vows, which have been widely taken, are wicked services of God and, consequently, are void. For a wicked vow, taken 40 against God's commandment, is not valid; for (as the Canon says) no vow ought to bind people to wickedness.

Paul says, "You are severed from Christ, 41 you who would be justified by the law; you have fallen away from grace" (Galatians 5:4). Therefore, anyone wanting to be justified by 42 his vows makes Christ useless and falls from grace. Anyone who tries to connect justifica- 43 tion to monastic vows bases his justification on his own works, which properly belongs to Christ's glory.

44   It cannot be denied that the monks have taught that they were justified and merited forgiveness of sins by means of their vows and observances. Indeed, they even invented greater absurdities, saying that they could

45   give others a share in their works. If anyone wanted to make more of this point, to make our opponents look even worse, even more things could be mentioned, things that even

46   the monks are ashamed of now. And on top of all this, the monks persuaded people that the services that they invented were a state of

47   Christian perfection. What else is this other

48   than assigning our justification to works? It is no light offense in the Church to set before the people a service invented by people, without God's commandment, and then to teach them that such service justifies. For the righteousness of faith, which ought to be the highest teaching in the Church, is hidden when these "wonderful" and "angelic" forms of worship, with their show of poverty, humility, and celibacy, are put in front of people.

49   God's precepts, and God's true service, are hidden when people hear that only monks are in a state of perfection. True Christian perfection is to fear God from the heart, to have great faith, and to trust that for Christ's sake we have a God who has been reconciled [2 Corinthians 5:18–19]. It means to ask for and expect from God His help in all things with confident assurance that we are to live according to our calling in life, being diligent in outward good works, serv-

50   ing in our calling. This is where true perfection and true service of God is to be found. It does not consist in celibacy or in begging

51   or in degrading clothes. The people come up with all sorts of harmful opinions based

on the false praise of monastic life. They   52 hear celibacy praised without measure and feel guilty about living in marriage. They   53 hear that only beggars are perfect, and so they keep their possessions and do business with guilty consciences. They hear that it   54 is an even higher work, a Gospel-counsel, not to seek revenge. So some in private life are not afraid to take revenge, for they hear that it is but a counsel and not a commandment. Others come to the conclusion that a   55 Christian cannot rightly hold a civil office or be a ruler.

There are on record examples of men   56 who hid themselves in monasteries because they wanted to forsake marriage and participation in society. They called this fleeing   57 from the world, and said they were seeking a kind of life that would be more pleasing to God. They did not realize that God ought to be served according to the commandments that He Himself has given, not in commandments made up by people. Only a life that   58 has God's commandment is good and perfect. It is necessary to teach the people about   59 these things.

Before our times, Gerson rebukes the   60 monks' error about perfection. He testifies that in his day it was a new saying that the monastic life is a state of perfection. So   61 many wicked opinions are inherent in monastic vows—that they justify, that they cause Christian perfection, that they make it possible to keep the counsels and commandments, that they are works over and above God's commandments. All these things are   62 false and empty. They make monastic vows null and void.

ARTICLE XXVIII

Church Authority

———

Note: Article XXVIII expands on Articles V and XIV. What authority, or power, do bishops have in the Church? Over the course of centuries, bishops had become not merely Church leaders, but political figures as well, claiming the right to govern both Church and State and to make and enforce laws in both realms. By returning to a biblical understanding of church, the Augsburg Confession clarifies that the true authority, or power, of bishops is the preaching of the Gospel, the forgiving and withholding of forgiveness of sins, and the administering of the Sacraments. The Church is not to interfere in the government, but is to keep its focus on the Gospel. This article is the foundation for the Lutheran understanding of the two kingdoms: God's work and rule in the world by means of the Church (the kingdom or regiment of the right hand) and the State (the kingdom or regiment of the left hand). Bishops, or pastors, have authority in the Church only to forgive sins in the name of Christ, to reject false doctrine and reprove those who uphold it, and to exclude persons who refuse to repent of open and manifest sin. This article, like the others, places the focus on the chief teaching of the Gospel: we are justified by God's grace through faith in Christ alone.

———

1 There has been great controversy about the power of the bishops, in which some have terribly confused the power of the 2 Church with the power of the State. This confusion has produced great war and riot. All the while the popes, claiming the Power of the Keys, have instituted new services and burdened consciences with Church discipline and excommunication. But they have also tried to transfer the kingdoms of this world to the Church by taking the Empire away from the emperor. Learned and godly 3 people have condemned these errors in the Church for a long time. Therefore, our 4 teachers, in order to comfort people's consciences, were constrained to show the difference between the authority of the Church and the authority of the State. They taught that both of them are to be held in reverence and honor, as God's chief blessings on earth, because they have God's command.

Our teachers' position is this: the au- 5 thority of the Keys [Matthew 16:19], or the authority of the bishops—according to the Gospel—is a power or commandment of God, to preach the Gospel, to forgive and retain sins, and to administer Sacraments. Christ sends out His apostles with 6 this command, "As the Father has sent Me, even so I am sending you . . . Receive the Holy Spirit. If you forgive the sins of anyone, they are forgiven; if you withhold forgiveness from anyone, it is withheld" (John 20:21–22). And in Mark 16:15, Christ says, 7 "Go . . . proclaim the Gospel to the whole creation."

This authority is exercised only by teach- 8 ing or preaching the Gospel and administering the Sacraments, either to many or to individuals, according to their calling. In this way are given not only bodily, but also eternal things: eternal righteousness, the Holy Spirit, and eternal life. These things 9 cannot reach us except by the ministry of the Word and the Sacraments, as Paul says, "The Gospel . . . is the power of God for salvation to everyone that believes" (Romans 1:16). Therefore, the Church has the 10 authority to grant eternal things and exercises this authority only by the ministry of the Word. So it does not interfere with civil government anymore than the art of singing interferes with civil government. For civil 11 government deals with other things than the Gospel does. Civil rulers do not defend minds, but bodies and bodily things against obvious injuries. They restrain people with the sword and physical punishment in order to preserve civil justice and peace [Romans 13:1–7].

12 Therefore, the Church's authority and the State's authority must not be confused. The Church's authority has its own commission to teach the Gospel and to administer

13 the Sacraments [Matthew 28:19–20]. Let it not break into the office of another. Let it not transfer the kingdoms of this world to itself. Let it not abolish the laws of civil rulers. Let it not abolish lawful obedience. Let it not interfere with judgments about civil ordinances or contracts. Let it not dictate laws to civil authorities about the form of so-

14 ciety. As Christ says, "My kingdom is not of

15 this world" (John 18:36). Also, "Who made Me a judge or arbitrator over you?" (Luke

16 12:14). Paul also says, "Our citizenship is

17 in heaven" (Philippians 3:20). And, "The weapons of our warfare are not of the flesh but have divine power to destroy strongholds" (2 Corinthians 10:4).

18 This is how our teachers distinguish between the duties of these two authorities. They command that both be honored and acknowledged as God's gifts and blessings.

19 If bishops have any authority of the State, this is not because they are bishops. In other words, it is not by the Gospel's commission. It is an authority they have received from kings and emperors for the purpose of administering the civil affairs of what belongs to them in society. This is another office, not the ministry of the Gospel.

20 Therefore, when a question arises about the bishops' jurisdiction, civil authority must be distinguished from the Church's jurisdic-

21 tion. Again, the only authority that belongs to the bishops is what they have according to the Gospel, or by divine right, as they say. For they have been given the ministry of the Word and Sacraments. They have no other authority according to the Gospel than the authority to forgive sins, to judge doctrine, to reject doctrines contrary to the Gospel, and to exclude from the communion of the Church wicked people, whose wickedness is known. They cannot exclude people with

22 human force, but simply by the Word. According to this Gospel authority, as a matter of necessity, by divine right, congregations must obey them, for Luke 10:16 says, "The

23 one who hears you hears Me." But when they teach or establish anything against the Gospel, then the congregations are forbidden by God's command to obey them.

Beware of false prophets. (Matthew 7:15)

24 But even if we or an angel from heaven should preach to you a Gospel contrary to the one we preached to you, let him be accursed. (Galatians 1:8)

25 For we cannot do anything against the truth, but only for the truth . . .

26 the authority that the Lord has given me for building up, and not for tearing down. (2 Corinthians 13:8–10)

27 The Canonical Laws also command this (II. Q. VII. Cap., *Sacerdotes*, and Cap.

28 *Oves*) And Augustine writes:

Neither must we submit to catholic bishops if they chance to err, or hold anything contrary to the canonical Scriptures of God. (*Contra Petiliani Epistolam*)

29 If the bishops have any other authority or jurisdiction, in hearing and judging certain cases, as of matrimony or of tithes, they have this authority only by human right. If the bishops do not carry out their duties in

these areas, the princes are bound, even if they do not want to, to dispense justice to their subjects in order to maintain peace.

30   There is also a dispute about whether or not bishops, or pastors, have the right to introduce ceremonies in the Church, and to make laws about meats, holy days, and grades, that is, orders of ministers, and so

31 on. Those who say that the bishops do have this right refer to this testimony of Christ in John 16:12–13, "I still have many things to say to you, but you cannot bear them now. When the Spirit of truth comes, He will

32 guide you into all the truth." They also refer to the example of the apostles, who commanded that Christians abstain from blood and from things strangled (Acts 15:[20,]

33 29). They refer to the Sabbath day as having been changed into the Lord's Day, contrary to the Decalog, as they understand it. In fact, they make more of the supposed change of the Sabbath day than any other example they can think of. They say that the Church's authority is so great, it has even done away with one of the Ten Commandments.

34   But on this question, for our part (as we have shown earlier) we teach that bishops have no authority to decree anything against the Gospel. The Canonical Laws

35 teach the same thing (Dist. IX). It is against Scripture to establish or require the observance of any traditions for the purpose of making satisfaction for sins, or to merit

36 grace and righteousness. When we try to merit justification by observing such things, we cause great harm to the glory of Christ's

37 merit. It is quite clear that by such beliefs, traditions have almost multiplied to an infinite degree in the Church, while at the same time, the doctrine about faith and the righteousness through faith has been suppressed. Gradually more holy days were made, fasts appointed, new ceremonies and services in honor of saints instituted. Those responsible for such things thought that by these works they were meriting grace. So 38 the Penitential Canons increased. We still see some traces of this in the satisfactions.

Those who establish such traditions are 39 acting contrary to God's command when they locate sin in foods, days, and similar things. They burden the Church with bondage to the Law, as if there needs to be something similar to the services commanded in Leviticus [chapters 1–7] in order to merit justification. They say that Christ has committed the arrangement of such services to the apostles and bishops. They have writ- 40 ten about the Law of Moses in such a way that the popes have been misled to some degree. This is how they have burdened the 41 Church, by making it a mortal sin—even if nobody else is offended—to do manual labor on holy days, or to skip the canonical hours, or that certain foods dirty the conscience, or that fasting is a work that appeases God. Or they say that, in a reserved case, sin can only be forgiven by the person who reserved the case, even though canon law speaks only of reserving the ecclesiastical penalty, not the guilt.

Who has given the bishops the right 42 to lay these traditions on the Church, by which they snare consciences? In Acts 15:10, Peter forbids us from putting a yoke on the neck of the disciples, and Paul says in 2 Corinthians 13:10 that the authority given to him was for edification, not for destruction. Why do the adversaries increase sins with their traditions?

There are clear testimonies that forbid 43 creating traditions in such a way as to suggest that they merit grace or are necessary to salvation. Paul says in Colossians 2:16, "Therefore let no one pass judgment on 44 you in questions of food and drink, or with regard to a festival or a new moon or a Sabbath." And later:

> If with Christ you died to the elemental spirits of the world, why, as if you were still alive in the world, do you submit to regulations—'Do not handle, Do not taste, Do not touch' (referring to things that all perish as they are used)—according to human precepts and teachings? These have indeed an appearance of wisdom. (Colossians 2:20–23)

46 Also in Titus 1:14 he openly forbids traditions with these words: "not devoting themselves to Jewish myths and the commands of people who turn away from the truth."

47 In Matthew 15:14, Christ says of those who require traditions, "Let them alone; 48 they are blind guides." In verse 13 He rejects such services: "Every plant that My heavenly Father has not planted will be rooted up."

49 If bishops have the right to burden churches with infinite traditions, and to snare consciences, why does Scripture so often forbid making and listening to traditions? Why does it call them "teachings of demons" (1 Timothy 4:1)? Did the Holy Spirit warn of these things in vain?

50 Therefore, ordinances instituted as though they are necessary, or with the view that they merit grace, are contrary to the Gospel. Therefore, it follows that it is not lawful for any bishop to institute and require 51 such services. It is necessary that the doctrine of Christian freedom be preserved in the churches. In other words, the bondage of the Law is not necessary in order to be justified, as it is written in the Epistle to the Galatians, "do not submit again to a yoke of 52 slavery" (5:1). It is necessary for the chief article of the Gospel to be preserved, namely that we obtain grace freely by faith in Christ, and not by certain observances or acts of worship devised by people.

53 What, then, are we to think of the Sunday rites, and similar things, in God's house? We answer that it is lawful for bishops, or pastors, to make ordinances so that things will be done orderly in the Church, but not to teach that we merit grace or make satisfaction for sins. Consciences are not bound to regard them as necessary services and to think that it is a sin to break them without offense to others. So in 1 Corinthians 11:5, 54 Paul concludes that women should cover their heads in the congregation and in 1 Corinthians 14:30, that interpreters be heard in order in the church, and so on.

55 It is proper that the churches keep such ordinances for the sake of love and tranquility, to avoid giving offense to another, so that all things be done in the churches in order, and without confusion (1 Corinthians 14:40; comp. Philippians 2:14). It is 56 proper to keep such ordinances just so long as consciences are not burdened to think that they are necessary to salvation, or to regard it as sin if they are changed without offending others. For instance, no one will say that a woman sins who goes out in public with her head uncovered, as long as no offense is given.

57 This kind of ordinance in the Church is observing the Lord's Day, Easter, Pentecost, and similar holy days and rites. It is a great 58 error for anyone to think that it is by the authority of the Church that we observe the Lord's Day as something necessary, instead of the Sabbath Day. Scripture itself has abol- 59 ished the Sabbath Day [Colossians 2:16–17]. It teaches that since the Gospel has been revealed, all the ceremonies of Moses can be omitted. Yet, because it was necessary 60 to appoint a certain day for the people to know when they ought to come together, it appears that the Church designated the

Lord's Day [Revelation 1:10] for this purpose. This day seems to have been chosen all the more for this additional reason: so people might have an example of Christian freedom and might know that keeping neither the Sabbath nor any other day is necessary.

61 There are monstrous debates about changing the law, ceremonies of the new law, and changing the Sabbath Day. They have all sprung from the false belief that in the Church there must be something similar to the services set forth in Leviticus [1–7], and that Christ had commissioned the apostles and bishops to come up with new 62 ceremonies necessary to salvation. These errors crept into the Church when the righteousness that comes through faith was 63 not taught clearly enough. Some debate whether or not keeping the Lord's Day is not a divine right, but similar to it. They prescribe the extent to which it is lawful to 64 work on holy days. What else are such disputes except traps for the conscience? Even when they try to modify the traditions, nobody will understand the modifications as long as the opinion remains that these traditions are necessary and must remain. There the righteousness of faith and Christian freedom is not known.

65 In Acts 15:20, the apostles commanded to abstain from blood. Who observes this now? Those who choose to eat blood do not sin, for not even the apostles themselves wanted to burden consciences with bondage to traditions. They forbid the eating of the 66 blood for a time to avoid giving offense. For in this decree we must always keep in mind what the aim of the Gospel is.

67 Scarcely any canon laws are kept with exactness. From day to day many go out of use, even among those who are the most zealous 68 advocates of traditions. In order to treat the conscience properly, we must realize that canon laws are to be kept without regarding them as necessary. No harm is done to the conscience even though traditions may go out of use.

69 The bishops might easily retain the legitimate obedience of the people if they would not insist upon the observance of traditions that cannot be kept with a good conscience. Instead, they command celibacy 70 and accept no preachers—unless they swear that they will not teach the Gospel's pure doctrine. The churches are not asking the 71 bishops to restore concord at the expense of their honor, even though it would be proper for good pastors to do this. They ask only 72 that the bishops release unjust burdens that are new and have been received contrary to the custom of the universal Church. It may 73 be that in the beginning there were plausible reasons for some of these ordinances, but they are not adapted to later times. It is also 74 clear that some were adopted through erroneous ideas. Therefore, it would be in keeping with the pope's mercy to change them now. Such a modification does not shake the Church's unity. Many human traditions have been changed over time, as the canons themselves show. But if it is impossible for 75 the adversaries to change those traditions, which they say is sinful to change, we must follow the apostolic rule, which commands us to "obey God rather than men" (Acts 5:29).

76 In 1 Peter 5:3, Peter forbids bishops to be lords and rule over the churches. It is not 77 our intention to take oversight away from the bishops. We ask only this one thing, that they allow the Gospel to be taught purely, and that they relax a few observances that they claim it is sinful to change. If they will 78 not give anything up, it is for them to decide how they will give an account to God for causing schism by their stubbornness.

Conclusion

1   These are the chief articles that seem to be in controversy. We could have mentioned more abuses. But here we have set forth only the chief points in order to avoid making this Confession too long. From these chief points 2 the rest may be easily judged. There have been, for example, great complaints about indulgences, pilgrimages, and the abuse of excommunication. Our parishes have been troubled in many ways by dealers in indulgences. There were endless arguments between the pastors and the monks about who has the right in parishes to hear confessions, do funerals, give sermons on extraordinary 3 occasions, and innumerable other things. We have passed over such issues so that the chief points in this matter, briefly set forth, 4 might be more easily understood. Nothing has been said or brought up for the rebuke 5 of anyone. We have mentioned only those things we thought it was necessary to talk about so that it would be understood that in doctrine and ceremonies we have received nothing contrary to Scripture or the Church universal. It is clear that we have been very careful to make sure no new ungodly doctrine creeps into our churches.

    We present these articles in accordance 6 with Your Imperial Majesty's edict, in order to show our Confession and let people see a summary of our teachers' doctrine. If there 7 is anything that anyone might desire in this Confession, we are ready, God willing, to present more thorough information according to the Scriptures.

Your Imperial Majesty's faithful subjects:	8
John, Duke of Saxony, Elector.	9
George, Margrave of Brandenburg.	10
Ernest, Duke of Lüneberg.	11
Philip, Landgrave of Hesse.	12
John Frederick, Duke of Saxony.	13
Francis, Duke of Lüneberg.	14
Wolfgang, Prince of Anhalt.	15
Senate and Magistracy of Nürnberg.	16
Senate of Reutlingen.	17

༄

UNDERSTANDING
INDULGENCES

——〜〜——

Note: The following is a translation of an actual indulgence administered in 1515 by
Albert, the Archbishop of Mainz and Magdeburg. It was designed to raise money for the
completion of St. Peter's Cathedral in Rome. It guarantees forgiveness and provides for the
reception of Communion, even when a person's territory was under a Communion ban
(interdict) by the pope. For example,

> Simply visit the church or churches of your choice on a day in Lent or an-
> other holiday . . . you will obtain as many indulgences and forgiveness of
> sins as if you had visited the church or churches in Rome on that same day.

During an interdict, a bishop or pope would not permit Masses to be said or any other
Sacraments to be administered in any churches of a given territory. Often interdicts were
issued whenever the monarch of a country defied Church authority. It was an effective
weapon used by the Medieval Church to keep monarchs in line. The common people, in
fear of dying outside of a state of grace, would frequently pressure their king to yield to the
Church's demands.

This sample indulgence is not part of the Book of Concord.

——〜〜——

We Grant Indulgence

Albert, by the grace of God and of the Apostolic See: Archbishop of Mainz and
Magdeburg, Administrator of the churches of Halberstadt, Primate of Germany,
Arch-Chancellor and Elector-Prince of the Holy Roman Empire, Duke of Mark
Brandenburg, Stettin, Pomerania, the Cashubians, and Slavs, Burggrave of Nürn-
berg, Prince of Rugia. Greetings in the Lord to those dear to us in Christ.

You have agreed to undertake an act of sincere and fervent devotion for the
Church of Rome. You have given to the building of the Basilica of St. Peter, an im-
mense undertaking requiring skillful production. Your contribution will not only
benefit that city, but it also shows that you are obedient to our commands.

Since you have given generously to our cause, you encourage and persuade us to
agree to [fulfill] your requests. You have long and fervently asked us that you might
have an altar stone on which Mass can be said. You have been looking for an altar
where Mass can be said without the meddling of foreign laws; we hereby grant your
request.

If you should happen to enter into regions placed under ecclesiastical interdict
by the authority of an ordinary bishop, nonetheless, you will not find yourself stand-

ing outside the doors of the church, excommunicated as it were. Instead, as long as you live, you will be able to celebrate Mass by yourself, if you are a priest. If you are a layperson, you may have Mass celebrated for you. You may use your own priest or any other priest. It does not matter whether the priest is a diocesan priest or a member of a religious order. This permission extends especially to the Easter Mass, even the Mass at sunrise. Of course, you may do this only if you yourself have not committed the sin that caused the land to be placed under the interdict.

You also may get as many indulgences and pardons for sin by visiting a church of your choice as if you had made a pilgrimage to Rome. Simply visit the church or churches of your choice on a day in Lent or another holiday when pilgrims visit the various churches around Rome. By taking a trip to a local church or churches, you will obtain as many indulgences and forgiveness of sins as if you had visited the church or churches in Rome on that same day.

You can also be given full Christian burial, even if you happen to die when your country is under an interdict. Of course, to receive this benefit you must not have committed the sin for which the land has been put under the interdict.

We issue this decree by the apostolic authority given to us by the letter "We Grant Indulgence," written by our Most Holy Lord Leo X, Pope by the grace of God. Nonetheless, please do not use a dispensation of this kind until the day you celebrate Mass or have it celebrated on your behalf. For when our Lord Jesus Christ (who is the radiance of eternal light) is being sacrificed in the liturgy of the altar, it is fitting that it not be done in the darkness of night but in the light. We order that the individual be communed into whose trust the present letter has been given and the seal has been affixed.

Date: In the year of our Lord 1515, on the _____ day of the month of _____, during the pontificate of our aforementioned lord, the Pope.

⚬⫘⚬

CONFESSIONAL SUBSCRIPTION:
AN EVANGELICAL ACT

Lutherans have always held that creeds and confessions are necessary for the well-being of the church. Just as Christ's church and all Christians are called upon to confess their faith (Matt. 10:32; Rom. 10:9; 1 Peter 3:15; 1 John 4:2), so the church, if it is to continue to proclaim the pure Gospel in season and out of season, must for many reasons construct formal and permanent symbols and confessions and require pastors and teachers to subscribe these confessions. It is impossible for the church to be a nonconfessional church, just as impossible as to be a nonconfessing church. And so today and ever since the Reformation Lutheran churches over the world have required their pastors to subscribe the Lutheran Confessions.

What does this mean? With her confessions the church is speaking to the world, but also to God, who has spoken to her in His Word—speaking to Him in total commitment, speaking to Him by an unequivocal, unconditional response in the spirit of, "We believe, teach, and confess" (FC Ep, Rule and Norm, 1). This response is Scriptural, taken from Scripture itself. How often do we read in our Confessions that the teaching presented is "grounded in God's Word"! And so the Confessions are no more than a kind of "comprehensive summary, rule, and norm," grounded in the Word of God, "according to which all doctrines should be judged and the errors which intruded should be explained and decided in a Christian way" (FC Ep, Heading). This would be an unbelievably arrogant position to take, were it not for the fact that all the doctrine of our Confessions is diligently and faithfully drawn from Scripture.

And so when the Lutheran pastor subscribes the Lutheran Confessions (and the confirmand or layman confesses his belief in the Catechism [LC, Preface, 19]), this is a primary way in which he willingly and joyfully and without reservation or qualification confesses his faith and proclaims to the world what his belief and doctrine and confession really are. Dr. C. F. W. Walther, the father of the Missouri Synod, long ago explained the meaning of confessional subscription, and his words are as cogent today as when they were first written. [From Walther's essay delivered at the Western District Convention, 1858.]

> An unconditional subscription is the solemn declaration which the individual who wants to serve the church makes under oath (1) that he accepts the *doctrinal content* of our Symbolical Books, because he recognizes the fact that it is in full agreement with Scripture and does not militate against Scripture in any point, whether that point be of major or minor importance; (2) that he therefore heartily believes in this divine truth and is determined to

preach this doctrine. . . . Whether the subject be dealt with expressly or only incidentally, an unconditional subscription refers to the whole content of the Symbols and does not allow the subscriber to make any mental reservation in any point. Nor will he exclude such doctrines as are discussed incidentally in support of other doctrines, because the fact that they are so stamps them as irrevocable articles of faith and demands their joyful acceptance by everyone who subscribes the Symbols.

This is precisely how the Confessions themselves understand subscription (FC Ep, Rule and Norm, 3, 5, 6; SD, Rule and Norm, 1, 2, 5).

Needless to say, confessional subscription in the nature of the case is binding and unconditional. A subscription with qualifications or reservations is a contradiction in terms and dishonest.

Today many Lutherans claim that such an unconditional subscription is legalistic. Sometimes they assert that such a position is pompous and not even honest.

We might respond: What can possibly be wrong about confessing our faith freely and taking our confession seriously? For it is the freest and most joyful act in the world for those of us who have searched these great confessional writings and found them to be Scriptural and evangelical to subscribe them. Of course, to force or bribe or wheedle a person into subscribing them would be an awful sin and a denial of what our Confessions are, namely symbols, standards around which Christians rally willingly and joyfully in all their Christian freedom.

From Robert D. Preus, *Getting into the Theology of Concord: A Study of the Book of Concord* (St. Louis: Concordia Publishing House, 1977), 15–16. For more information, see *Doctrine Is Life: Robert D. Preus Essays on Justification and the Lutheran Confessions* (St. Louis: Concordia Publishing House, 2006), 195–212.

The Luther Rose

The Luther Rose is the most well-known symbol of Lutheranism.
Here is how Martin Luther explained it:

First, there is a black cross in a heart that remains its natural color. This is to remind me that it is faith in the Crucified One that saves us. Anyone who believes from the heart will be justified [Romans 10:10]. It is a black cross, which mortifies and causes pain, but it leaves the heart its natural color. It doesn't destroy nature, that is to say, it does not kill us but keeps us alive, for the just shall live by faith in the Crucified One [Romans 1:17]. The heart should stand in the middle of a white rose. This is to show that faith gives joy, comfort, and peace—it puts the believer into a white, joyous rose. Faith does not give peace and joy like the world gives [John 14:27]. This is why the rose must be white, not red. White is the color of the spirits and angels [cf. Matthew 28:3; John 20:12]. This rose should stand in a sky-blue field, symbolizing that a joyful spirit and faith is a beginning of heavenly, future joy, which begins now, but is grasped in hope, not yet fully revealed. Around the field of blue is a golden ring to symbolize that blessedness in heaven lasts forever and has no end. Heavenly blessedness is exquisite, beyond all joy and better than any possessions, just as gold is the most valuable and precious metal. (Letter to Lazarus Spengler, July 8, 1530 [WABr5:445]; trans. P. T. McCain)